T0114565

Global Delicacies

Diversity, Exotic, Strange, Weird, Relativism.

Andrew Nyakupfuka

BALBOA.
PRESS
A DIVISION OF HAY HOUSE

Balboa Press books may be ordered through booksellers or by contacting:

Balboa Press
A Division of Hay House
1663 Liberty Drive
Bloomington, IN 47403
www.balboapress.com
1-(877) 407-4847

Because of the dynamic nature of the Internet, any web addresses or links contained in this book may have changed since publication and may no longer be valid. The views expressed in this work are solely those of the author and do not necessarily reflect the views of the publisher, and the publisher hereby disclaims any responsibility for them.

The author of this book does not dispense medical advice or prescribe the use of any technique as a form of treatment for physical, emotional, or medical problems without the advice of a physician, either directly or indirectly. The intent of the author is only to offer information of a general nature to help you in your quest for emotional and spiritual well-being. In the event you use any of the information in this book for yourself, which is your constitutional right, the author and the publisher assume no responsibility for your actions.

Any people depicted in stock imagery provided by Thinkstock are models, and such images are being used for illustrative purposes only.
Certain stock imagery © Thinkstock.

Printed in the United States of America

ISBN: 978-1-4525-6790-7 (sc)
ISBN: 978-1-4525-6791-4 (e)

Balboa Press rev. date: 03/29/2013

Table of Contents

Introduction.

NUTRITIONISTS AND HEALTH OFFICIALS believe that we are what we eat. I wonder if they ever thought of some foods or drinks we consume in the name of delicacies. I believe that delicacies may be some food we eat or drink for pleasure, they may not be part and parcel of our daily diet therefore they may not be compatible with nutritions' assertion on whom we are. Delicacies could be defined by culture, religion, and socioeconomic status or personal taste and flavor around the world. We normally do not eat delicacies every day. I believe delicacies are consumed at special occasions such as at weddings, initiation ceremonial rituals, and tourism trips or other important gatherings. What one culture considers a delicacy could be disgusting to other people. Eating of one particular food once in a while may not define who we are health wise although it could be true culturally. The most important thing about delicacies is that we must not be judgmental on what other people eat. We should respect and educate ourselves on why some people eat certain foods other than what we eat.

I have selected a few delicacies the world over in this contribution as some points for discussion. A delicacy can be defined broadly as any food item that is considered highly desirable in certain cultures because of its flavors, characteristics or because of its scarcity. For example the ivory king salmon is highly valued because of its scarcity. Any scarce food item attracts a high price at the food market. By virtue of its prohibitive price a certain type of food may automatically become a delicacy, for example some seafood like crab, lobster, prawns and shrimp. Alternatively, a delicacy could be any food item which is foreign to a certain culture is considered a delicacy, for example Zimbabweans consider salad as a delicacy because it was introduced by the British colonialists. Salad is not part of the Zimbabwean diet. A delicacy could also be determined by its food texture for example caviar is considered to be royal food in Russian and Asian cultural and political circles. Delicacies are different, controversial and subjective globally. Delicacies could be weird and strange depending on one's culture and taste. They can only fit in the adage,' One man's meat is another man's poison.' I am going to list down some delicacies particularly in Zimbabwe and its neighbors, some Asian countries, Latin American countries as these countries have similar trends of delicacies. I will also include some delicacies in some western countries. I am going to cite a short history of each delicacy, texture, and method of how to prepare it, as well some benefits particularly medicinal ones and suggest some best fit recipes in Zimbabwe and from the internet.

I was motivated to give this contribution because the world is now a global village, people travel some very long distances in the shortest time. People move around the world quickly and may be amused about what they see other people eating in the name of a delicacy or part of their diet. I have to equip both immigrants and tourists with some delicacies information so that they should not cringe when they see some people from other parts of the globe eat certain kinds of food and why they eat that kind of food. For example horse/donkey meat (stracotto d' asino) and frog legs are delicacies in France while some Africans in general shun such kind of meat. Americans have among their delicacies such as prime beef, Maine lobsters, Maryland blue crabs, Morel mushroom and many others. The British have the following list food items as delicacies in their chest of drawer, bacon roll with brown sauce, haggis, and digestive biscuits, fruit Muesli from Tesco, short bread, and cream tea, steak, Guinness pie and many others. It is unheard of to eat dog as a delicacy in many parts of the world but the Chinese do. People from Tamil Nadu in the Indian peninsula eat snake meat while Zimbabweans dread snakes because of their venom. Some Zimbabweans and people from neighboring countries eat offal, some edible insects such as Mopani worms, stink bugs, and rodents such as mice, squirrel, rabbit, and many others .Crocodile tail, and pig brain are some of the exotic delicacies in Zimbabwe. The idea of eating crocodile tail is foreign and it came from Australia and South Africa. It is taboo to eat crocodile in Zimbabwe. The Philippines eat balut as a delicacy while some cultures around the globe find that practice as offensive and distasteful.

Reptiles.

REPTILES ARE A LARGE group of cold bloodied animals which also include amphibians. Reptiles are those animals with scales/scutes covering their skin. Reptiles include crocodiles, alligators, and snakes, lizards, tortoises, and turtles, terrapins, and gavials, tuatara and caimans. However, amphibians are those reptiles with two lives, which is they can both live on land and in water. They generally include frogs and toads. The term reptile is only an umbrella term. There are some differences and similarities among its members. For example some reptiles such as some snakes can also live both on land and in water for example pythons. The majority of reptiles reproduce by internal fertilization and they lay their eggs on land while amphibians reproduce by means of external fertilization and they lay their eggs in water. Their eggs hatch into tadpoles while reptiles' eggs hatch into young ones which are similar to their parents. Both reptiles and amphibians do not feed or look after their young ones. All reptiles have a three chambered hearts except the crocodile which has a four chambered heart like mammals.

Humans all over the world have developed an appetite and taste to eat the meat of both reptiles and amphibians as part of their main diet or delicacy. Those selected for consumption include crocodiles, alligators, and some snake species such as the python, cobra, anaconda and many others. Lizards such as the monitor lizard and iguana have not been spared either. Turtles and tortoises ,frogs and toads are also eaten. People have chosen to eat all the meat cuts of reptiles or have chosen to eat some particular parts. For example, the crocodile tail is a delicacy to Zimbabwean tourists. Some of the reptile body parts selected for consumption include the loin and legs. It is believed that some crocodile's body parts have medicinal values while the skins have been turned into leather to make expensive clothes such as coats, shoes, and belts as well as trinkets or cultural ceremonial outfits. I am made to believe that some crocodile bones are used by fortune tellers and witchdoctors in their trade.

Crocodile Tail.

Crocodiles are biologically more closely related to birds and dinosaurs than to reptiles for example crocodiles have four chambered hearts as earlier on alluded to. Crocodiles were once perceived as the river gods in African folklore just as snakes were to the Chinese. The crocodile is known by different names according to Zimbabwean dialects. It is known as "ngwena, garwe or ngwenya." Some Zimbabweans have totems aligned to the crocodile for example all people who have the surname 'Ngwenya' in the Ndebele language belong to the crocodile totem. It is taboo to eat crocodile if one's totem was "crocodile" among the Shona people. However, the Ndebele an off shoot of the Zulu tribe in South Africa have a different culture from the Shona. They might eat crocodile if they choose to. Myth has it that crocodile meat is poisonous particularly the bile although there is no scientific proof. It is believed that some locals used crocodile bile for witchcraft purposes; for example they could sprinkle the bile into someone's food particularly beer, hence some Zimbabweans used to burn the whole crocodile carcass should they capture or kill a crocodile. Crocodiles are ferocious reptiles. They feed by grabbing and holding onto their prey, they have sharp teeth for tearing and holding onto flesh, and powerful muscles to close the jaws and hold them shut. These jaws can bite down with immense force. Crocodiles are patient ambush hunters, waiting for fish or land animals to come close, and then rushing out to attack. Crocodiles feed on fish, birds, and mammals as well as carrion. Crocodiles are also cannibals. They also eat their young ones when there is scarcity of food. Crocodiles swallow stomach stones which may act as ballast to balance their bodies or assist in crushing food, similar to grit in birds.

Zimbabwe is home to the Nile crocodile, the largest of all crocodile species in the world. Crocodile tail fillet is served in elite hotels and restaurants in Zimbabwe as a delicacy or exotic food. It is believed that crocodile tail fillet is surprisingly tender and delicious. Some people say that crocodile tail fillet is similar to veal in texture but tastes like chicken, rabbit, fish or frog's legs. Some come up with different crocodile tail fillet taste options and say that crocodile tail fillet tastes like white portions of pork. I am also told that some prefer crocodile feet which they say taste like frog's leg hence they call them crocodile wings. Crocodile meat is regarded as exotic in some circles and it is used for making hamburgers or hot dogs. Crocodile meat is also considered healthier than chicken. Crocodile meat is slowly coming to Zimbabweans dinner tables, thanks to global influence and education that crocodile meat is safe to eat. I am yet to taste crocodile tail fillet due to some conservative ideologies. Crocodile meat is mostly consumed in Australia, China, and Southeast Asia while elite Americans eat alligators particularly the tail fillet.

Chinese physicians believed that dried crocodile meat was a good natural treatment for asthma patients. They would prescribe dried crocodile meat to be boiled with some herbs and drink the water. However, some patients boiled crocodile meat in water with a bit of some salt and it worked. It was their belief that when we eat meat of animal we take some of that animal's qualities. They believed that crocodile meat strengthens the lungs because a crocodile could stay submerged for longer periods. Some asthma patients still use this asthma treatment today. I read about a Singaporean woman who used crocodile meat asthma natural treatment and she was cured. It is further believed that crocodile meat is a cure for rheumatism, anemia, and diabetes, cancer and expels dampness as well as making bones strong. The Chinese also believed that regular consumption of crocodile meat promoted the physical wellbeing by improving the body's immune system. However, some doctors disputed such natural cure prescriptions.

Zimbabweans are not only breaking away from the taboo of not eating crocodile meat but have also found some commercial values of crocodile farming. Zimbabwe has some commercial crocodile farms dotted around the country, the biggest being in Kariba and Victoria Falls. Locals are being introduced to crocodile farming around the country to boost the economy and their livelihood. Crocodiles are reared and harvested in Zimbabwe mostly for their skin products which are used as leather for making some expensive shoes, belts, and handbags for export. Crocodile meat is mostly consumed in Australia, China, and Singapore while elite Americans eat alligators.

Crocodile meat can be prepared in many forms, the simplest being loins, tail and body. Crocodile is a white meat with a nutritional composition comparing favorably with that of more traditional meats, for example chicken. As meat is a secondary product, it is generally prepared according to specific government orders. Crocodile meat is low fat, low cholesterol, a good alternative to red meat such as beef and game. Crocodile meat has a delicate flavor, so the use of strong marinades is not recommended. Light tropical fruits compliment crocodile meat well.

GRILLED CAJUN STYLE CROCODILE TAIL.

Ingredients.

  4 to 6 pounds of crocodile tail

  Lemon wedges

  12 teaspoons paprika

  6 teaspoons powder garlic

  3 teaspoon white pepper

  3 teaspoon Oregano, crushed

  2 ½ teaspoons black pepper

  1 teaspoon cayenne pepper

  Seasoning mix

Directions.

1. To make seasoning mix, combine paprika, garlic powder, salt, white pepper, oregano, black pepper, thyme and cayenne pepper in jar with tight fitting lid.
2. Shake well to combine. Mixture may be stored for up to 3 months.
3. When ready to cook, cut gator tail meat into 1/2" cubes. Roll each cube in 1 tablespoon of the mixture.
4. Cook over high heat on an outdoor barbecue grill or under the oven broiler for 4 to 6 minutes, or until crocodile tail meat is white and firm to the touch.
5. Serve warm with lemon wedges. The seasoning mixture will coat up to 24 (4 oz.) servings of crocodile tail.

Monitor Lizards.

Monitor Lizard or Bayawak. (Tsamba, Mupurwa)
Lizards have white meat which is low in calories.
Lizard meat tastes like native chicken

Monitor lizards including their cousin the iguana are found in most tropical regions of the world. They are revered as delicacies in Central America particularly in El Salvador where they are now commercially raised for export to such countries as the United States. Lizards are also big business in Vietnam and other South Asian countries. (Ast 2003) states that monitor lizards are diurnal reptiles which mean that they are active during the day. Monitor lizards have elongated necks and forked tongues. They have dark colorations with various yellow spots .Monitor lizards use their long forked tongues when hunting to sniff out their prey. However, they do not have taste buds. Monitor lizards have a pair of apical horns. Monitor lizards are generally carnivores feeding on small mammals, birds, fish, and carrion. Other species of the monitor lizards are vegetarians feeding mainly on fruit, flowers, and leaves. Monitor lizards produce by sexual reproduction. They are both terrestrial and aquatic creatures. However, most of them are found on terrestrial habitats such as burrows, surface, living among rocks, or arboreal. There are two different types of monitor lizards in Zimbabwe namely," mupurwa or tsamba and hukurutumbo or gwavava."The former leaves in wetlands and sometimes hunt in water while the later is found in rocky places. I do not have any knowledge of current practices of eating monitor lizards in Zimbabwe. But that does not mean that people do not eat monitor lizards. I am told that monitor lizards were my grandfather's and other people of his age delicacy. He preferred monitor lizard meat to chicken or goat meat. He would exchange his most treasured goat for a monitor lizard. The recipe was simple; he used to kill and skin the monitor lizard and smoked it overnight on low heat. His first wife was always assigned to cook the monitor lizard. She could stew the lizard meat and mix it with peanut butter. It is generally believed that Monitor lizards have white meat which is low in calories and tastes like native chicken, hence the name "hukurutombo" literally meaning mountain or rock chicken. Due to environmental degradation, overpopulation, and climate change the monitor lizard habitat and population has been greatly depleted in most parts of Zimbabwe.

Monitor Lizard meat is not only a delicacy but it is also cherished for its medicinal properties such as asthma and general cough natural cure and as an aphrodisiac though there is no scientific proof to substantiate these claims. The bones are so hard that some local people in Sri Lanka use them to beat their drums at special ceremonies and rituals. The skins or pelts are used as leather to make belts, handbags, and other trinkets.

Iguana.

Iguana is an inclusive name for several large lizards species found in tropical America in countries such as Mexico, Brazil, Central America, and the Caribbean. The common iguana is arboreal and strictly vegetarian feeding on fruit flowers and leaves. They are mostly found along streams and rivers. Iguanas generally have tall flat plates jutting from their back like spines; they also have a rough skin. The green iguanas are bright green in color with dark stripes on the tail. However, some green iguana species are dull - green or grayish – green in color. They also have a crest of spines which runs from the neck to the tail. Iguanas have excellent vision and can see colors and movement at long distances. Iguanas use their eyes to navigate through crowded forest for food or predators. They also use visual signals to communicate with other members of the same species. The meat and eggs of the common iguana are prime delicacies. An iguana lays all her eggs at a single sitting. They can lay up to fifty to sixty eggs. They require specific weather and temperatures to successfully lay a clutch of eggs hence it is sometimes difficult to lay eggs in captivity. Iguanas are also excellent pets but very difficult to keep in captivity because it is difficult to create a conducive environment for their up keep such as a warm and fairly humid place. The iguana population in Zimbababwe is severely depleted because their habitat is being destroyed by climate change, over population and agricultural activities as people and iguanas compete for land use. Most iguanas can found in zoos and in homes. There are different ways to prepare and cook iguanas and monitor lizards meat and eggs .Below are some selected recipes.

Traditional Recipes.

Iguana Pazole.

Ingredients.
   2 medium iguanas
   5 cups of freshly bleached hominy
   10 cloves of garlic
   1 onion
   1 slice of cabbage, diced
   Bay leaf
   Mexican oregano
   Salt, pepper and corn

Instructions.
1. Butcher, skin and cut the iguana in pieces.
2. Wash, salt and blanch for 15 -20 minutes.
3. Simmer the corn, garlic, bay leaf, and salt to taste for 10 minutes.
4. Cook for another 15 -20 minutes.
5. Serve with sliced cabbage some of the onion slice, cilantro, oregano and pepper to taste.

Iguana (Hukurutombo): Iguana meat is also known as "bamboo chicken" or "chicken from the trees."
Photographer: Konstantin Krismer.

Iguana Recipe.

IGUANA ROASTED WITH BIRRIA MARINADE

Ingredients.
   8 guajilo chili
   2 passila chili
   4 cloves garlic
   Oregano vinegar
   Salt pepper to taste

Instructions.
1.   Butcher, skin and cut the iguana into pieces.
2.   Wash, salt and blanch for 15 -20 minutes.
3.   Toast and soak the peppers.
4.   Blend the soaked chili with vinegar, oregano, salt and pepper to taste.
5.   Marinate the iguana meat in the mixture for at least 2 hours.
6.   Roast the iguana at high heat (450 deg F) until tender.

Iguana Eggs

Ingredients.
    Italian brad crumbs
    Whole jalapeno peppers.
    Cream cheese
    3 iguana scrambled eggs
    Canola oil

Directions.
1. Remove the seeds from the peppers without breaking it open. This can be done with a paring knife. Wash the pepper out well.
2. Fill the inside of the peppers with cream cheese.
3. Roll them around on paper towel to dry them off, and dip them in the egg. When they are covered with egg, roll them in the bread crumbs until covered.
4. Fry the iguana eggs in the oil until golden-brown.

Snake Meat.

Zimbabweans dread all types of snakes, poisonous or not. Most snake species are nonvenomous except for some of the cobra and viper species. Snakes bite to kill and not for self defense. Some snakes kill their prey by constricting for example the python and anaconda. Zimbabweans kill any type of snake on sight. They believe that all snakes are poisonous, though scientifically that is not true. Furthermore some snake species like the python and cobras are believed to be used by witches and wizards to cause harm to some perceived foes. It is believed snakes used for witchcraft purposes are kept as pets. Folklore has it that snakes are agents or merchants of witchcraft and bad luck. Some Zimbabwean Christians do not like snakes because they believe that a snake is the mother of all sins and the snake represents all that is evil. They drive this assertion from the story of Adam and Eve in the Garden of Eden. (Genesis 3). There are no snake charmers in Zimbabwe. Some people are actually scared to see snakes in movies or in pictures. It is unthinkable and a taboo to eat snake meat in Zimbabwe. Due to the shortage of beef and bush meat I suspect some Zimbabweans may experiment in eating snake meat. I base my theory in the fact that people of different cultures and tribes now live side by side today .However; I was also made to believe that some people of the Malawian origin do eat snake meat. It is believed that some Malawians who stayed and worked on Zimbabwe's commercial farms ate snake meat. It was believed that these people used to engage in black magic using snakes, owls, hyenas and sundry for example in their cultural dances called" Gure". I was surprised to hear a co-worker from Peru saying that they eat snake meat. That sent some shivers down my spine. I tried by all means to look for snake meat in American grocery stores but I found none. I was told that I could get snake meat in mini market shops for people of Central American origin. I just want to see snake meat and examine its texture. Although Zimbabweans generally do not eat snake meat I urge them to respect those who do. Zimbabweans have their own bizarre or strange delicacies as we shall see later.

The Chinese respected the snake in the same way Zimbabweans respected the crocodile as both reptiles were revered as river gods but these two culturally and spiritually respected (gods) reptiles ended up in some dinner plates as delicacies.Newman Jacqueline M. (2000) in her article, "Snakes as Food and Medicine" stated that the Chinese have a love-hate relationship with snakes and in the past used to worship them; as river gods were often imagined in the form of snakes as were animal demons. The love-hate relationship is also because snakes represent all that is negative in the world of superstition and yet are regarded as clever but wicked.

However, the Chinese and other cultures in the Far East, India, and Latin America consider snake meat as a delicacy. Snake meat is also consumed as a delicacy in some parts of India, for example in some Tamil Nadu districts where the black rat, blue rat and yellow rat snakes are hunted and killed for their meat. Indians also engage and kill the most venomous cobra species. They use some sticks to draw out snakes from their hide outs or dig them out from holes. Indian snake hunters and snake charmers are taught the trades at a tender age of about six years of age. Indians slaughter the snakes and remove their pelts using some blades. They do not eat snake offal such as the head, gut, and intestines. Indians from the above mentioned district will swear to you that snake meat is edible, very tasty, and delicious. They claim that snake meat has some curative properties. They use snake meat as pain relievers, joint, and cough treatment.

Nutritionists and pharmacists have also established that snake meat contains proteins, calcium, magnesium, and other elements which prevent cardiovascular diseases and osteoporosis. Snake meat contains about 93 calories per 100 grams of raw snake meat depending on the type of a snake. It is also documented that snake meat is good for dieters and weight watchers because snake meat controls their weight since it contains half of the calories and a third of the amount of fat in beef steak. It has been proved scientifically that snake meat has supplement blood, enhances strong bones, and muscles, beauty, and nourishes the skin. It is further alluded to that in clinical practice snake meat is suitable for rheumatic artharalgia, skin diseases, bone and joint tuberculosis, scrofula, numbness and peripheral nerve palsy consumption. Below are some snakes which have found themselves in dinner plates in different parts of the world.

Rattlesnake.

Rattle snakes are one of the most dangerous and poisonous snakes in the world. The rattlesnake is characterized by some rings at tip of the tail. The rattling sound is meant to warn its foes that they are approaching a dangerous territory and that they should back off. However, rattlesnakes rarely bite unless provoked or threatened. They bite to kill and often for food and rarely as self defense. Rattlesnake meat is considered an exotic cuisine in America and other parts of the world. People have different tastes and opinions on rattlesnake delicacy. Taste options are usually driven from the recipe. Some people who have eaten rattlesnake meat say that it is very tough and chewy while others declare that rattlesnake meat tastes like chicken. People have different tastes opinions as regards rattlesnake meat. Some people may eat rattlesnake as a snack. Therefore rattlesnake meat taste is controversial and subjective. I am yet to see anyone eating rattlesnake.

Rattlesnake meat is believed to be a widespread Hispanic folk remedy in its dried form. It can be offered in an array of recipes, such as rattlesnake fajita pitas to deep-fried and served with coleslaw. Rattle snake meat is considered a delicacy in some American southwest states restaurants, these states include Texas, Oklahoma, New Mexico, and Arizona and others. However, rattlesnake meat whether consumed as a delicacy or as a novelty, should never be eaten raw, even when offered dried. Rattlesnake should be thoroughly washed particularly over running water before cooking. Be warned that raw rattlesnake meat carries rare, yet potentially deadly parasites and has been documented to infect humans with salmonella bacteria so thorough cooking is imperative. Below are some suggested rattlesnake recipes.

Rattlesnake Recipe.

RATTLESNAKE FAJITA PITAS.

Ingredients.
- 1 rattlesnake, filleted and cut into small pieces
- Olive, to sear meat
- 6 cherry tomatoes, halved
- Guacamole
- 3 tablespoons teriyaki sauce
- 1 large bell pepper
- 6 onion flavored pita bread packets
- 1 teaspoon seasoned salt (recommended Lawry's brand).
- 1 large onion sliced
- Sour cream
- 1 teaspoon jalapeno seasoning
- ½ clove garlic, minced
- Picente sauce
- Cheese Vegetables

Directions.
1. Marinate rattlesnake meat, refrigerated, for about 3 hours in teriyaki sauce, seasoned salt and jalapeno seasoning.
2. In a large iron skillet, heat olive oil and sear meat.
3. Add bell pepper, onion, garlic and tomatoes and cook for about 10 minutes until vegetables are tender.
4. Add any additional seasonings to suit taste. Cut pitas in 1/2 and butter the inside of the pocket and toast until crispy.
5. Spoon rattlesnake meat and vegetables into pitas and top with cheese.

6. Served best on a bed of rice with side condiments of picante sauce, guacamole and sour cream.

Source. Tod and Elaine Ryden.

Rattlesnake meat recipe.

How to Prepare the Rattle Snake.
1. Decapitate the head about 4 inches from the neck.
2. Hang the rattle snake by the tail.
3. Cut the belly of the rattle snake from end to end in a straight line.
4. Once you make the incision the meat and the inside of the rattle snake easily separate from the meat.
5. Remove all of the insides and internal organs of the rattle snake.
6. Wash the rattle snake thoroughly using cold water.
7. Cook the rattle snake over campfire.
8. If you prefer rattle snake meat without bones, then they will become easy to remove after a short while on the fire pit.

Source: Rodney Southern. A Yahoo Contributor.

Python.

Pythons are docile and colorful reptiles found in many different parts of the world which include India, Africa, China and Southeast Asia, Europe and America. They are often killed on the assumption that they are dangerous as other snakes. They are also killed because they kill domestic animals such as dogs, chickens, goats and sheep. Pythons are nonvenomous.They kill their prey by constriction. They only bite as self defense. Pythons are facing extinction because their habitat is being destroyed for land usage which includes home construction and agriculture. Python meat is considered a delicacy in the Far East and parts of the Middle East, and China. Pythons are also captured and exported to some developed countries such as the United States of America where they are kept as pets although they become extremely dangerous as they grow. Owners may release these pets or they escape from captivity. They are becoming a nuisance in the everglades swamps in Florida.

Pythons are held in esteem in Chinese medicinal folklore, it is believed that python meat purifies our blood; cure such diseases as arthritis and some skin diseases. There is also an assertion that python meat can be used as a warming food ingredient with the blood often mixed with liquor to produce a virility enhancer. Python meat has a delicate chicken flavor and should be cooked thoroughly as it is not suitable for raw consumption.

Python (Shato, Tsato). Python skin can be used as leather
to make shoes, handbags, and belts. Zimbabweans use
the skin for ceremonial rituals and python fat is used
as love potions by witchdoctors.They believe that the
intended partner would be as docile as a python.
Photographer: Mariluna.

How to Cook Python Meat.

Ingredients.

Obtain a python from a trusted source or familiar environment; avoid the risk of eating a snake that has eaten a poisoned rodent.

1 box of cornbread mix

½ egg whites

Splash black pepper

½ inch oil (depends on pan size)

Instructions.

1. Refrigerate the python carcass as soon as possible. It can also be frozen. The meat's integrity remains intact, and the coloration of the skin is unaffected. Skin the snake.

2. Cut off the head, strip off the skin, and remove the guts of the dead python.

3. Rinse the meat, and cut it into pieces with a sharp knife or poultry shears. Make the cuts between and at the same angle as the ribs to avoid cutting the ribs.

4. If the ribs are severed, they may be difficult to remove from the meat after it is cooked. Some people prefer to soak the ready-to-cook snake pieces in saltwater for a day or two to remove any remaining blood or "gaminess" from the meat.

5. Dip the segments in a bit of egg white (milk would also do) before dredging them in a pepper and sweet cornmeal mix (or cornbread mix with some extra black pepper.)

6. Heat about 3/4" (2cm) of canola, vegetable, or peanut oil in a heavy frying pan until quite hot. Add the snake pieces one at a time to avoid from dropping the temperature in

the pan too quickly. Use tongs to keep your fingers away from the sizzling hot oil, watch for dangerous splatters, and use a screen if necessary to prevent a mess.

7. Turn the snake pieces just as the butter begins to turn golden - by the time it starts to brown the snake will be overcooked. There's not much meat on the bones, and the muscles are thin and lean.

8. Serve your fried snake bites warm, and provide napkins as this is a finger food. Accompany with almost anything you would serve with fried fish.

Turtle.

Turtles are found throughout the world particularly in the temperate and tropical regions as well as in the open ocean. Edible turtles include marine and green turtles, diamondback terrapin, and soft – shelled turtles. It is believed that about forty- two percent of these rare turtles face extinction because of over harvesting .Catching of female turtles when they lay eggs on land has also accelerated the turtle extinction process. Turtles lay between one (100) hundred to two (200) hundred eggs in a clutch. They use their flippers to dig some pits to lay their eggs. Green turtles are herbivores feeding on sea grasses while their juveniles may feed on jellyfish and sponges while other turtle species are carnivores. Young turtles are threatened by predators such as crabs and sea gulls on their journey from the nest to the sea. Turtles are also threatened by boat propellers, fishing nets, and their nesting grounds are being destroyed by human encroachment. Turtles are considered a delicacy in Japan, China, the Far East, and America as well as the Caribbean Islands.

There is a variety of tortoise species across southern Africa from the Indian to the Atlantic oceans .These tortoise species include the leopard, hinged or hingeback, ungulate and pygmy or padlopers. They are found in different climate regions from the savanna, karoo and temperate regions in South Africa, semi desert and desert in Namibia as well as the Okavango swamps in Botswana. Tortoises feed on a variety of plant materials which include berries and fruit. However the leopard tortoise was also observed feeding on semi dry elephant dung and whitish-colored spotted hyena's droppings or human feces. Most people in southern Africa eat tortoise meat as part of their diet or as a delicacy. Zimbabwe is a landlocked country therefore turtle meat is imported and only served in elite restaurants and hotels. However, Zimbabwe has a small number of tortoises in its ranches and national parks and zoos. Zimbabwe's tortoise also faces extinction because of over harvesting and poaching. Its habitat is being destroyed for home construction as people are encroaching into some conservatives and wild fires. Tortoise population is also threatened by the ever increasing Chinese population who consider tortoise meat as a delicacy. There have been some court hearings over the Chinese who were stealing small tortoises from zoos. It is also believed that the Chinese can pay some rural folks handsomely for collecting tortoises especially near conservatives. The tortoise, especially the young is also threatened by predators such as lions, leopards and hyenas.

Most Zimbabweans do not generally eat tortoise meat, but the old generations do. I think this is by choice because there are no cultural restrictions from eating tortoise meat, or because there is a lot of bush meat to choose from. Some people can swear to you that turtle meat and eggs are an exotic delicacy. It is also believed that turtle meat tastes like frog legs or lobster. Turtle meat is popular in stew, gumbo and soups. I have never eaten tortoise or turtle meat before. In countries such as Singapore with large Chinese populations, turtle soup is a delicacy. The meat, skin and innards of the turtle are used as soup. Soft-shelled turtles are commonly consumed as soup in Chinese cuisine, while consumption of hard-shelled turtles is often avoided due to their mythical connotations. However, the hard shells of certain turtles are used in the preparation of "turtle jelly." Turtle jelly is made by boiling the shells into a jelly substance. The water is allowed to evaporate from the substance to create the jelly. Chinese culture believes that turtle jelly flushes out toxins from the body and can also treat cancer and insomnia. Just like in other reptile meat medicinal properties, turtle meat is used for treating cardiovascular diseases, anemia, and weakness due to chemotherapy. Brazilians use turtle fat to treat ear ache, rheumatism, and sore throat. The Chinese also believe that eating turtle helps in the enrichment of blood and provides a cooling effect to the body. It is believed that turtle meat particularly the bones improves the male's virility.

I understand that some Zimbabwean witchdoctors, charlatans, and sorcerers sometimes use tortoise shells and bones in casting lots in fortune telling (hakata) and treatment for certain ailments such as malnutrition. I have often seen babies wearing some sort of necklaces with a small turtle, tortoise or snail shell. It is believed that that shell protects babies from weight loss. Zimbabweans believe that since shells are a hard, they protect the child from weight loss. That turtle/snail/oyster shell necklace practice is popularly known as "nyengerekezi" in the Shona culture. Alternatively they may bathe or make their babies drink some water with some tortoise/snail/ oyster shells aiming to achieve the same results – protection from weight loss.

Turtle Recipes.

Turtle Soup.

Ingredients.
1 ½ sticks of butter
1 tablespoon dried thyme, ground
1 tablespoon hot pepper sauce
2 ½ pounds of turtle meat cut into medium dice
2 quarts veal stock
¼ cup Worcestershire
Salt and freshly cracked pepper
1 cup all purpose flour
2 large lemons, juiced
2 medium onions, cut into medium dice
6 medium hard- boiled eggs, chopped into large pieces
10 ounces fresh spinach stems removed, washed 3 times, and
   roughly chopped.
30 cloves garlic, minced
6 stalks celery, cut into medium dice
3cups peeled, chopped, and seeded tomatoes
3 bell peppers cut into medium dice
1 table spoon dried thyme, ground 26 ounces dry sherry
   (750 ml bottle)

Directions.

Cook's Note: We use alligator snapping turtles, which are a farm-raised fresh water species available all year long. Turtle meat usually comes in 2 1/2-pound portions.

1. In a large soup pot over medium to high heat, melt 1/2 stick butter.

2. Add turtle meat and brown. Season, to taste, with salt and pepper.

3. Cook for about 18 to 20 minutes or until liquid is almost dry.
4. Add onions, celery, garlic, and peppers, constantly stirring.
5. Add thyme, oregano, and bay leaves and sauté for about 22 minutes**.
6. Add stock, bring to a boil, and simmer for 30 minutes. Skim any fat that comes to the top.
7. While stock is simmering, make the roux. In a small saucepan, melt remaining butter over medium heat.
8. Slowly add flour, a little at a time, constantly stirring with a wooden spoon. Be careful not to burn.
9. After all of the flour has been added, cook until roux smells nutty, is pale in color, and has a consistency of wet sand, about 3 minutes.
10. Set aside to let cool until soup is ready (roux should be cool when adding to hot soup).
11. Using a whisk, stir the roux into the stock vigorously, adding a little at a time to prevent lumping.
12. Simmer for about 25 minutes. Stir to prevent sticking on bottom.
13. Add sherry and bring to a boil.
14. Add hot sauce and Worcestershire sauce. Simmer and skim any fat or foam that comes to top.
15. Add lemon juice and tomatoes and return to a simmer.
16. Add spinach and eggs return to a simmer and adjust seasoning.

Edible Insects.

ENTOMOPHAGY, IS THE PRACTICE of insect eating, it is a growing industry globally. Entrepreneurs are making insects both palatable and marketable and in turn profitable. These innovations are adding another income source for farmers and the poor, and supplying another weapon to the battle for global food security. Chavunduka (1975) noted that in several areas of Zimbabwe, some families make a fairly good living from selling caterpillars while Conconi (1982) proposed the 'industrialization' of all edible insects in Mexico. It has been proved scientifically that insects are very high in protein, all forms of vitamin B; mineral salts such as iron and zinc. It has been proved that insects are much easier to rear than livestock and they produce less waste. Three companies in the Netherlands have embarked in insect production and they have found the venture to be highly profitable. These farms includeWageningen University Research farm and Kreca VOF. It is fact that insects are always available in abundance than livestock or game. Based on the weight of the food required to feed them, crickets are twice as efficient as pigs and broiler chicks, four times more efficient than sheep and six times more efficient than cows. They breed at a far faster rate. They are seen as an ecologically friendly alternative to traditional animal rearing.

However, insects have a reputation for being dirty and carrying some diseases yet it has been documented that less than 0.5% of all known insect species are harmful to humans, farm animals or crop plants. Harmful insects may include female anopheles mosquitoes, ticks, and houseflies as well as cockroaches. Some cultures all over the world eat some selected insects as delicacies; these include Mopani worms, locusts, and stinkbugs, cicadas, and scorpions, cockroaches (roaches), and termites and many others.

Humans derive some other benefits from insects such as medicinal, cosmetic and industrial properties. For example bees provide us with bee pollen, beeswax, and royal jelly, propolis, and organic honey, and bee bread. Bee pollen helps plants in the crops cross pollination process. Bee pollen is different from other forms of pollen which cause some allergies. Bee pollen is low in calories, but rich in proteins, amino acids, vitamins, and enzymes. It is also antibacterial, ant-viral and helps in lowering cholesterol. Bee pollen stabilizes and strengthens capillaries. Bee pollen rejuvenates the body and stimulates organs, enhances vitality and the rate of recovery which makes it popular with sportsmen. Bees wax is also used in skin care products, candles, and furniture polish, as well as batik making. Royal jelly contains vitamins B5 and B6 and amino acids which are a potent antioxidant, a special rejuvenating substance that promotes tissue growth, muscle and cell regeneration.Propolis helps us in climate changes. It is antibacterial, antiviral, anti –inflammatory. It has been scientifically proved that bee bread promotes kids' physical and mental growth which includes memory. It also helps in weight gain and fights obesity. Bees' digestive enzymes are used for treating, anemia, hepatitis, and insomnia, stress, failing memory, cholesterol and digestive tract disorder.

Some insects products can be used to dye our foods such as the red dye cochineal in imitation crab sticks, Compari, and candies. Humans may not consume silk worms but get a lot of benefits from silk worm larvae for example; silk worms provide us with silk which we get from silk worm cocoons which we in turn use in the linen industry. Silk worms have some medicinal properties, for example we use dried silk worms for treating spasms and flatulence .Silk worm extract contain unsaturated vitamins, proteins, amino acids as well as cephalin which is used in the treatment of a variety of ailments such as migraine, carpal tunnel syndrome, and osteoarthritis, rheumatoid arthritis, and fibromyalgia, and the curing of skin lesions, and prostate hyperplasia. It is also believed that extracts from dried male silk moths are used as an aphrodisiac.

Spiders are used as effective fly control agents in our homes while spider venom is now transformed in new technologies as pain relief, anti –venom, and stroke treatment, as well as erectile dysfunction. Spider venom is also used to clot blood and produce faster healing. Spider silk is used in cross – hairs microscopes, telescopes, rifle sights, as well as in optics. It has been proved that spider silk is superior to synthetic materials because it is light, strong and elastic hence scientists are contemplating to insert spider silk genes into mammals and plants in order to produce much stronger materials. Cicada larvae on the other hand tunnel through the soil and aerate plant roots, they also eat organic matter and break up debri.It is also believed that cicadas are a great source of fertilizer. Cicadas have short lives, when they die; their bodies quickly break down into nitrogen and other nutrients that plants can use. Cicadas are also an integral part of the animal food chain.

Zebra Mopani Worm (Mshonja, Madora, Mabayamukanwa, Amathsimbi).Mopani worms are harvested for both profit and nutrition in Southern Africa.

ANDREW NYAKUPFUKA

In Zimbabwe, (Matabeleland North and South Provinces) edible insects are a multimillion dollar industry, as well as a delicacy. Mopani worms are seasonal butterfly larvae prevalent in (SADC) which include Zimbabwe, South Africa, and Botswana, Namibia, and Zambia. Mopani worms are harvested for profits and nutrition. The worms, which inhabit Mopani or mango trees, require only three kilograms of feed (Mopani/mango leaves) to produce one kilogram of worms. Mopani worm varieties in Zimbabwe and neighboring countries include emperor moth. They are also known as "gonimbrasia belina madora/amathsimbi/omangungu in different local languages. The worms (larvae) are usually boiled and then sun dried by locals. The local people are being trained in how to harvest the worms hygienically, and how to sort and grade them. The Mopani worm products include deep-fried snacks and seasoning spices. Mopani worms can also be found in cans soaked in brine.

It is critical that Mopani worms are harvested in a sustainable way, because in some parts of southern Africa, Mopani worms have been driven into extinction. However, most local people including some teachers do not fully comprehend the life cycle of the Mopani worms. They do not understand that once you break one stage of the cycle, the worms will go extinct. Some locals have this archaic theory that they can re –introduce Mopani worms by performing a traditional ritual whereby they would scatter the ashes from the fires used for preparing the worms for market in the affected areas where the Mopani worms were harvested. Some environmental activists believe that it was feasible to relocate some larvae and eggs to some unaffected Mopani woodlands and then breed them in captivity. The Mopani worms are also threatened by the cutting down of the Mopani trees in order to harvest worms. The cutting down of Mopani trees is also accelerating the desertification process in the affected areas.

Preparing Mopani Worms.

Caterpillars are prepared for eating by squeezing out the gut contents before they are fried in their own body fat or boiled in a little water. Most of the caterpillars are dried so that they can be stored for use throughout the year. Dried caterpillars may be eaten dry as a snack or rehydrated and cooked in a little water before they are fried in oil with onion and tomato. They may be served with pap (maize meal porridge), onion and tomato gravy and at char (chili sauce). Mopani worms' nutritional values consist of about 60% crude protein, 17% crude fat, and 11% minerals, on a dry matter basis. Mopani worms are also believed to aid HIV/AIDS patients with the necessary nutrients in their diet.

Mopani Worms Recipe.

DRIED MOPANI WORMS STEW.

Ingredients.
   Tomatoes
   Onion
   Peanut sauce
   Salt to taste

Directions.
1. Prepare tomato and onion stew or "dovi."
2. Soak for a few hours in water.
3. Add to your tomato and onion stew or "dovi" peanut sauce.
4. Cook through.
5. Serve with sadza/vhuswa.

Source: True Love Cookbook.

Edible Desert Locust.

Locust (Hwiza,Mhashu, Dzomba): Jewish Kosher Dietary Laws permit the consumption of locusts. However, kosher dietary laws prohibit the consumption of any other insect.

Locusts are a type of insect from the family "Acrididae" and are also known as grasshoppers. Locusts swarm in huge numbers and can travel long distances, causing considerable damage to crops. However, in many African, Middle Eastern and Asian countries, locusts are considered a delicacy and eaten in abundance. Locusts are an excellent source of protein and contain a variety of fatty acids and minerals. Although not considered palatable by most Americans, locusts are an important food source in many other countries including Zimbabwe. According to the book, "Insects" by Steve Parker, species of locusts vary in protein content from about 50 percent of dry weight to almost 60 percent, making them denser in protein than cows. However, the protein of some species of locust is not considered complete because it lacks the essential amino acid methionine, which cannot be made by human beings.

Overall, the protein nutritional value of locust is considered inferior to casein, which is the primary protein of dairy products.

The percentage of fat in desert locusts is lower than their percentage of protein, but still a reasonable source, at almost 12 percent, according to a 2001 edition of the "Journal of King Saud University." The percentages of saturated and unsaturated fatty acids are 44 percent and 54 percent, respectively. Palmiteic, oleic and linolenic acids are the most abundant fatty acids. However, the researchers noted that the cholesterol content in locusts is high, about 286 milligrams per 100 grams, which is higher than that found in beef or poultry. Locusts also contain adequate amounts of iodine, phosphorus, iron, thiamine, riboflavin, niacin, as well as traces of calcium, magnesium and selenium. Carbohydrate levels are very low in locusts, which makes them a good candidate for Atkins and Paleo types of diets. Some people describe cooked locust as similar to smoky flavored bacon and reasonably tasty. Americans advised to exercise caution if they are in a foreign country and willing to try locusts, as their sanitary practices are seldom to the standards of the United States of America.

Although locusts can be considered a delicacy, they can also be a devastating pest causing severe damage to crops, pastures, and vegetables, as well as orchard crops. It is believed that a swarm of locusts can eat up to ten tonnes of vegetation per day. There is also this funny story that a certain family in Kenya realized a huge profit after harvesting a swarm of locusts which had destroyed their millet crop. The family could not have realized that fortune had the swarm not destroyed their crop. In other words that was a blessing in disguise. I was made to believe that some environmentalists are training some refugees on how to catch locusts so that they can supplement protein in their diet as there is a shortage of beef. Locusts are also a nuisance in Australia where they were reported to have caused a crop loss of more than five million dollars. If you are a Christian you very well know the eighth out of ten plagues (Exodus 10: 1 -20) ,the Plague of the Locusts. The plague of the locusts was designed to show God's superiority over the Egyptian gods. It was also meant to put pressure on Pharaoh to release the Israelites from bondage. The locusts swarmed all of Egypt. The locusts nimbled all the crops, pastures and leaves which were left after the hail .However, although Kosher dietary laws forbid the eating of insects, locusts are an exception.

Green Grasshopper.

Green grasshopper, "Tsunyatsunya /Dhumbuhla" in my local language is a seasonal hopper. It is commonly seen during the rainy season. The hoppers forage in green grass or green leaves of crops such as rice, corn, and millet, or wheat .Women and children collect grasshoppers using their bare hands very early in the morning when the temperature is very low, and hoppers can hardly fly. Grasshoppers have five eyes but no ears. The five eyes make it very difficult to catch them. Hoppers see in all directions. If you have ever tried to catch a grasshopper you have seen firsthand how very hard it is. That is because all of these eyes allow a grasshopper to see not only long distances, but also forwards, backwards and sideways.

Urbanites in Zimbabwe catch grasshoppers at street lights in the evening as they are attracted to lights. Green grasshoppers are also considered a delicacy in Uganda; where they are called "nsenene". Green grasshoppers are roasted and winnowed to remove the wings then fried using very little cooking oil if any, as they have enough oil in their bodies and salted. Fried green hoppers can be eaten as a snack or consumed with "sadza". Some women sell them at their market stalls or at pub entrances as they go very well with beer. If you decide to eat grasshoppers do not eat them raw. They need to be cleaned and cooked. If not, you could end up with a tapeworm. In the United States of America and other Western countries, grasshoppers are sometimes coated with chocolate and considered a delicacy.

How to cook grasshoppers.

1. Get the grasshoppers from nearby farms or plains using a net. (You can buy grasshoppers in some Mexican grocery shops if you stay in the United States of America.)
2. Boil the grasshoppers in a stock pot.
3. Marinate the boiled grasshoppers in lemon juice with smashed garlic and some salt for an hour.
4. Drain the lemon juice, but not too much, you need to keep some moisture.
5. Keep on cooking until you smell the ingredients in the air.
6. Taste the hoppers and keep on shaking them until they have the taste you want. Be careful not to burn them
7. Serve as a snack.

Edible Ants.

Hormiga Culona.

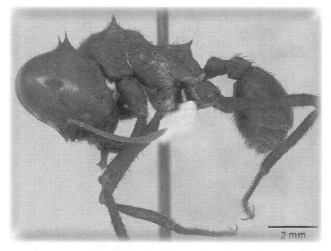

Hormiga Culona (Bachaco/Big Bottom Ant,
"Dendemafuta, Tsambarapfuta"). It is said that roasted
hormiga culona tastes like buttered popcorn.
Photographer: April Nobile.

Hormiga Culona.

THE "HORMIGA CULONA," OR big-butt queen ant, also known as
(Tsambarapfuta or dende mafuta) in Zimbabwe is eaten straight
up with salt. It can also be roasted using very little water as the
butt is full fat and dried in trays. Some Zimbabwean women sell
Hormiga Coluna in their market stalls or at beer hall entrances as

Hormiga Coluna is a popular snack with ale drinkers. Hormiga Coluna is also a delicacy in Columbia's Santander province. The culonas are a source of cultural pride and epicurean delight in Columbia. Hormiga Coluna is a seasonal delicacy. This ant is fried and eaten in the Santander region of Colombia. It is said that the colonna's taste is similar to peanuts. Locals catch the culonas using traps they set on anthills or collect them on street lights in urban areas as they are attracted to lights in the evening.

Termites.

People have eaten termites in many different cultures around the world for time immemorial. Africa in particular seems to be the centre of termite eating. The alates and macro termite soldier have been an important component in the diet of native African populations. Different tribes have different methods of collecting or even cultivating the insects, though some also collected the soldiers of some species. Queens are harder to come by, but are widely regarded as a delicacy when available. Workers and soldiers care for the eggs and young. Worker and soldier termites are, sterile, blind and sometimes they are polymorphic.The alates are certainly nutritious, having a good store of fat and protein, and are palatable in most species with a nutty flavor when cooked. They are easily gathered at the beginning of the rainy season when they swarm, as they are attracted to lights and can be gathered up when they land on nets put up around a lamp. The wings are shed and can be removed by winnowing. They are best gently roasted on a hot plate or lightly fried until slightly crisp; oil is not usually needed since their bodies are naturally high in oil. Traditionally they make a welcome treat at the beginning of the rainy season when livestock is lean, new crops have not yet produced food, and stored produce from the previous growing season is running low

In other continents termites are also eaten, though generally more locally or tribally in some parts of Asia and the Americas than in Africa. In Australia the aboriginal people knew of termites as being edible, but apparently they did not relish them greatly, even in hard times. It is unclear from most sources whether the lack of interest extended to the alates as well as the workers and soldiers

Soldier Termites.

Soldier termites have elongated brown heads, extra big jaws, or sometimes chemical sprays to use on enemies of the nest. Soldier and worker termites defend the nest. Zimbabweans also eat soldier termites. Soldier termites can be cooked or eaten raw. Many local tribes in Africa have been known to take soldier termites and cook them over an open flame, in a sautéed fashion. They make a great afternoon snack and have a nutty flavor once fried.

Scorpion.

Photographer: Chris Huh.
Asian Forest Scorpion (Rize/Mhani/Chinyaride):
Scorpions are a delicacy in many Asian countries
including China, Vietnam, and Taiwan.

Scorpions are found all over the world particularly in deserts, tropical forests, and rock crevices. Scorpions are scientifically closely related to spiders, mites, and ticks. They are also burrowing insects particularly in areas permafrost or where the grass is heavy.

ANDREW NYAKUPFUKA

Scorpions can also be found under the bark of firewood. I used to experience some scorpion stings when collecting firewood. They are dreaded for their ferocious sting and venom capable of killing a human being. Scorpions are predatory animals, feeding mostly on insects. They have eight legs, a pair of front grasping claws and a narrow segmented tail often carried in a forward curve over the back and ending with a venomous stinger. The scorpion is part of the Chinese zodiac dating back to the Babylonian astronomers. In North Africa and South Asia the scorpion is a cultural animal. It is believed that the scorpion portrays homosexuality. There is nothing scientifically or traditionally to substantiate this assertion .Scorpions are used in folk medicine in South Asia especially in antidotes for scorpion stings. Scorpions are a delicacy in China and other Asian countries. Scorpions can be eaten alive, deep fried or in soups. However, some people discourage the practice of eating raw insects. It is believed that insects carry some harmful parasites, such as bacteria. Americans and other people the world over cringe seeing someone eat a scorpion in whatever form. Chinese chefs empty the venom out before cooking them. Those who have eaten scorpion say that scorpion tastes like any sea food like shrimp, crab, or lobster.Nutritions have documented that scorpions have the following nutritional values, fat 1.1%, carbohydratetes 96.7%, and proteins, 2.2%.

Though Zimbabweans dread scorpion stings, scientists are researching and developing methods of making scorpion venom useful to humans. It has been proved that scorpion venom can be successfully used in heart transplant, boosting the immune system, and treatment for rheumatoid arthritis. It is also believed that scorpion venom can be used in preventing cancer cells from spreading. It can also be used as a pain killer as well as a pest control.

Scorpion Recipes.

SCORPION BOWL.

Ingredients.
- 3 cups crushed ice
- 2 fluid ounces gin
- 2 fluid grenadine syrup
- 8 fluid ounces orange juice
- 1 fluid ounce dark rum
- 10 ounces pineapple juice
- 2 fluid ounces 151 proof rum
- 3 fluid ounce fresh lemon juice (optional)
- 2 fluid light rum
- 4 pineapple chunks

Directions.
1. Place the crushed ice in a large pitcher and pour in the gin, dark rum, 151 proof rum, light rum, vodka, grenadine, orange juice, pineapple juice, and lemon juice.
2. Stir well to mix.
3. Pour into a large, decorative cocktail glass.
4. Garnish with pineapple, cherries, and straws.

Scorpion Bowl.

Ingredients.
- 1 ounce brandy
- 1 ounce light rum
- 3 ounces unsweetened pineapple juice
- ½ ounce orgeat
- Dash grenadine
- ¼ cup dark rum

Instructions.
1. Shake all ingredients with ice; then strain over ice into a chilled highball glass.

Salad with Chipotle-Dusted Fried Scorpion & Aloe Vinaigrette.

Ingredients.

- 2 cups scorpion
- 1 regular orange juiced
- 1 tablespoon Wondra flour
- 2 large carrots
- 4 tablespoon cilantro, chopped
- 2 large oranges
- 2 limes, juiced
- ½ cup Extra Virgin Olive Oil
- ¼ cup pumpkin seeds
- 1 teaspoon cumin

Method.

1. Add chipotle powder to flour, dredge scorpions in flour mix and fry in deep fryer until crispy- about 3 minutes.
2. On a Mandolin, julienne carrots. Cut blood orange supremes.
3. Make a dressing with orange and lime juice, extra virgin olive oil and cumin.
4. In a bowl mix shaved carrots, orange segments and cilantro.
5. Dress with vinaigrette.
6. Serve fried scorpions on top on the salad, sprinkle with pumpkin seeds

Cicada.

Cicadas are distinguished by their stout bodies, broad heads, and large compound eyes as well as clear – membrane wings. They are best known for their buzzing and clicking noises. Cicadas are also famous for their penchant for disappearing entirely for many years and only to appear in force at a regular interval. The cicada is considered as a pricy delicacy in some cultures around the world for example in China, Cambodia, and Thailand, Vietnam, Burma, and Indonesia and the world over. Some people say that cicadas taste like asparagus or calm – flavored potato. However, some cultures and religions such as Jews and Moslems do not eat insects including the cicada .Most Zimbabweans do not eat cicadas but I understand a very small section of the population do eat them, particularly in the low veldt such as the Zambezi valley where they appear in their millions. It is also suggested that birds, dogs, and cats, spiders, and snakes feast on the cicada bonanza. Cicadas are seasonal insects prevalent in spring. Cicadas are low in fat and high in protein. Some people mistakenly view cicadas as locusts, but locusts are migratory grasshoppers that often travel in large swarms destroying crops and pastures in their wake. Early European settlers in North America equated cicadas with the plague of locusts mentioned in the Bible because cicadas can be found in large numbers, however, they were wrong. Cicadas are aligned with some cultural and social themes such as resurrection, immorality, spiritual realization and spirituality ecstasy. It is believed that ancient Greeks and Romans considered cicadas as sacred and sang in intoxicated ecstasy imitating cicadas in praise of Apollo. Cicadas had also some religious significance in China. They symbolized reincarnation or immortality. The Chinese compared cicadas periodic molting of their shells with a person's living leaving the physical body behind at the time of death.

Cicadas have some medicinal importance in the Chinese scientific and traditional fields; these include the treatment of fevers associated with seizures, skin rashes, and eye disorders such as conjunctivitis, cataracts, and blurred vision. Cicadas are also associated in the treatment of high fevers such as the common cold or influenza. It is also believed that the combination of cicada and silkworm droppings may treat fevers associated with SARS (Severe Acute Respiratory Syndrome).Cicadas are also associated with the treatment of the following diseases or conditions; laryngitis, headache, and restless sleep or nightmares. Cicadas are also associated with the treatment of a variety with spasms such as the early stages of measles or chickenpox, and reducing muscle tension of the striated muscles.

Cicada Recipes.

HONEY (UCHI).

Honey can be defined as a sweet and viscous fluid produced by bees and other insects from the nectar of flowers. The flavor and color of the substance is largely determined by the type of the flowers from which the nectar is gathered. Common flavors of honey include orange blossom honey, tupelo honey, clover honey, blackberry, and blueberry honey.Honey has a long history of human consumption, and is used in various foods and beverages as a sweetener and flavoring. It also has a role in religion and symbolism. In Hinduism, honey is one of the five elixirs of immortality. In temples, honey is poured over the deity. In Jewish tradition, honey is a symbol for the New Year, "Rosh Hashanah". At the traditional meal for that holiday, apple slices are dipped in honey and eaten to bring a sweet new year. In Buddhism, honey plays an important role in the festival of "Madhu Purnima", celebrated in India and Bangladesh. The day commemorates Buddha's making peace among his disciples by retreating into the wilderness. In Australia, Tasmanian leatherwood honey is considered a delicacy for its unique flavor. "Manuka" honey from New Zealand is said by some to have more healing properties than other honeys, therefore sells at a premium price. Similar to honey, and usually bottled and sold as honey is honeydew, which is made by the bees from the sweet secretions of aphids, scale, or other plant sap sucking insects. Honeydew from pine forests has a "piney" taste and is prized for medicinal use in Europe and Turkey. A side-effect of bees collecting nectar and pollen to make honey is pollination, which is crucial for flowering plants

Commercial bee keeping in Zimbabwe is mostly found on commercial farms. Most Zimbabwe rural folk engage in harvesting wild honey mostly for their own consumption. However, those who engage in bee keeping use some primitive or makeshift bee hives made from the bark of trees which they shape in a cylinder shape (mukoko).They use some rolled dry grass to close both ends of the cylinder leaving small vents where bees can enter and exit the cylinder. They may also access honey from crevices or in anthills tunnels (guru) made by termites. They may suspend the makeshift bee hive on tree branch or put it in between branches for support. They use the primitive ways of harvesting honey. Although honey is a delicacy to most Zimbabweans, it comes with a price to those who harvest the honey as the African (killer bee) bee is a vicious defender of its honey and grubs. Honey harvesting is mostly done at night though some daring honey harvesters do it during the day, at a heavy price though. They do not have modern equipment for harvesting honey; all they need is native grass to burn and smoke out the bees. They produce a rich dense, cool smoke to make the bees docile. However, African bees are stubborn they may not relent or yield to the smoke and sting the smoker viciously. In some cases the smoker may abandon the exercise and run away for dear life. Zimbabwean bee harvesters use their bare hands to take out the honey from the bee hive and put into a container. Most Zimbabweans eat little honey because of its high price, scarcity and the dangers of harvesting it, making honey a delicacy. Those who have access to honey usually eat it raw or they use it make some cake called "chambwa".

The main uses of honey are in cooking, baking, spreading on bread or toast, and adding to various beverages such as tea. Because honey is hygroscopic, a small quantity of honey added to a pastry recipe will retard it from becoming stale. Raw honey also contains enzymes that help in its digestion. It also contains several vitamins and antioxidants. Honey is also used in traditional folk medicine. It is an excellent natural preservative. Honey is, however, not always healthy. Because it is gathered from flowers in the wild, there are certain times and places when the honey produced are highly toxic. Honey does not spoil. Because of its high sugar concentration, it kills bacteria by osmotically lysing them. Natural airborne yeasts cannot become active in it because the moisture content is too low. Natural, raw, honey varies from 14% to 18% moisture content. As long as the moisture content remains under 18% nothing will grow in honey.

How to Use Medicinally.

Instructions.

1. Treat a cough and sore throat by giving the sufferer I teaspoon. of honey with a squeeze of lemon juice as needed. Honey kills bacteria in the throat and relieves a cough.

2. Apply honey to minor (and major) burns to kill bacteria and speed healing of the wound faster than normal means. Using honey to aid burns also lessens scarring upon healing.

3. Make up a hot drink with I tablespoon of honey, I teaspoon of lemon juice and I teaspoon. of apple cider vinegar to aid in weight loss. Drink everyday for maximum effect.

4. Apply sparingly as a diaper rash ointment to kill bacteria and germs, speeding healing of baby's bottom.

5. Mix honey with whipped egg white and apply to face as a scrub to eliminate bacteria and grease.

6. Treat leg ulcers with honey to halt infection, kill bacteria, or heal with less scarring.

7. Apply to athlete's foot as you would with antifungal creams or spray. Honey's antifungal properties kill fungus naturally.

Honey Ribs.

Ingredients.
  10.5 ounces beef broth
  3 tablespoons honey mustard
  ¼ cup water
  ¼ honey barbeque sauce
  ¼ cup soy sauce
  ¼ cup maple syrup
  3 pounds baby pork ribs

Directions.
1. In the crock of a slow cooker, mix together the beef broth, honey mustard, honey, water, barbeque sauce, soy sauce, and maple syrup.
2. Slice ribs apart, leaving an even amount of meat on each side of the bone.
3. Place them into the slow cooker so that they are covered by the sauce. If there is not enough sauce, you may add a little water or beef broth to compensate.
4. Serve.

How to Brew Mead.

Instructions.

Glass 1 – gallon jug
1 gallon of spring water
3 pounds honey
1 air lock
1 rubber stopper (solid)
1 rubber stopper with a hole in it so you can place the airlock
A mixing bowl
Yeast energizer (white container with brown label)(1 teaspoon)
Yeast nutrient (white container with blue label) (1 teaspoon)

Directions.

1. Put about 1/3 to 1/2 gallon of spring water into your 1 gallon glass carboy and then add your three pounds of honey.
2. Add the Energizer and Nutrient
3. Pour two cups of spring water into your glass mixing bowl and add 1 teaspoon of energizer and 1 teaspoon of nutrient to it. Stir it up well and add it to the honey and water mix
4. Put the solid rubber stopper on the bottle and shake the mead mix gently to get it homogenous
5. Heat two cups of spring water on the stove to between 104 and 109 degrees Fahrenheit. This is warm and not hot. If this water gets too hot you will kill the yeast

6. Clean your mixing bowl while you are waiting for the water to heat. Then when the temp of the water is right pour it in your mixing bowl then pour 1/2 of a package of yeast into the water. Do not stir it yet. Just pour it in and wait 15 minutes. When the 15 minutes is up give it a gentle stir so everything is homogenous then pour it right into your jug of honey water

7. Now add more spring water to the jug until it is full. You will have left over spring water because the honey has taken up some space in the jug of course. It should be 1 gallon when it looks about like this picture here. To make sure of where the one gallon full mark was I had originally poured a full gallon of spring water in the jug and made a mark with a marker. Just so I could be sure of what the one gallon mark was. Now I just filled to that mark.

8. Put the rubber stopper on your bottle and shake it vigorously for five full minutes. And at intervals take the cork off to let it breathe then continue shaking. It is important to shake it well for five full minutes because this aerates the must. This aeration is important for the growth of the yeast.

9. Fill the airlock about half full of water, put it through the rubber stopper then put it firmly on the bottle.

Spider (Dzwatswatswa).

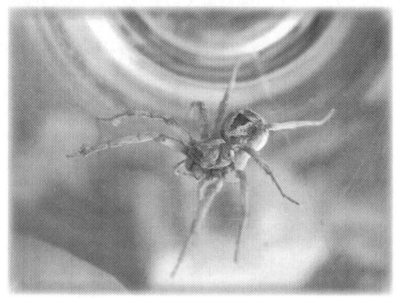

Spider meat taste has been described as bland,
"rather like a cross between chicken and cod.

Spiders belong to the same biological family as mites, ticks, and daddylong legs and scorpions. Spiders have eight legs with claws at the end of each leg and mouth parts with fangs that inject venom which quickly kills or paralyses their victims. Spiders have eyes and book lungs which enable them to see and breathe. Spiders are found on every continent. They are predators, mostly preying on insects and cannibals. It has also been observed that a few large species of spiders take on birds and lizards. Spiders use a wide range of strategies to capture prey by trapping it in sticky webs, mimicking the prey to avoid detection, or running it down. Most spiders detect prey mainly by sensing vibrations, but the active hunters have acute vision and those which hunt show signs of intelligence in their choice of tactics and ability to develop new ones. Spiders' guts are too narrow to take solids, and they liquidize their food by flooding it with digestive enzymes and grinding it with the bases of their pedipalps. It is interesting to note that male spiders identify themselves by a variety of complex courtship rituals to avoid being eaten by the females. It has been observed that males of most species survive a few matings, because they have a short life or they can be eaten by the female spiders. Females weave silk egg-cases, each of which may contain hundreds of eggs. While the venom of a few species is dangerous to humans, scientists are now researching on the use of spider venom in medicine and as non-polluting pesticides. Spider silk provides a combination of lightness, strength and elasticity that is superior to that of synthetic materials, and spider silk genes have been inserted into mammals and plants to see if these can be used as silk factories. Some cultures have found solace in eating spiders as delicacies.

It is taboo to eat spiders in Zimbabwe in any form. However, spiders are a delicacy in China and the Far East in countries like Cambodia, Vietnam, and Indonesia, the Philippines and Thailand. Fried spider is a regional delicacy in Cambodia and its taste has been described as bland, a cross between chicken and cod with a contrast in texture from a crispy exterior to a soft center. The legs contain little flesh, while the head and body have a delicate white meat inside. Some people do not seem to enjoy the abdomen, because it contains a brown paste consisting of organs such as eggs, and excrement. However, others call the abdomen the most delicious part of the spider.

ANDREW NYAKUPFUKA

Recipes.

Fried Spider.

THE SPIDERS ARE TOSSED in a mixture of, sugar, and salt; crushed garlic is fried in oil until fragrant, then the spiders are added and fried alongside the garlic until "the legs are almost completely stiff, by which time the contents of the abdomen are not so runny. The taste has been described as bland, "rather like a cross between chicken and cod, with a contrast in texture from a crispy exterior to a soft centre. The legs contain little flesh, while the head and body have a delicate white meat inside. There are certainly those who might not enjoy the abdomen, however, as it contains a brown paste consisting of organs, possibly eggs, and excrement. Some call it a delicacy while others recommend not eating it.

Cockroaches.

Cockroaches are considered a delicacy in Asian countries including China. Cockroaches are biologically related to termites and praying mantises. Most of them are generally dark in color that is they could be black, brown, or reddish; some of the them have some unique markings. Cockroaches are most common in tropical and subtropical climates. Some species are in close association with human dwellings and widely found around garbage or in the kitchen while others could be found in the wild and usually in caves, sewers and old mines or burrows. Cockroaches are generally nocturnal; however some are diurnal or both. They can run quickly or fly. Cockroaches are generally omnivorous. It has been scientifically proved that cockroaches carry a variety of funguses, harmful bacteria's, and parasitic worms which cause some diseases to humans for example, leprosy, bubonic plague, and dysentery, diarrhea, urinary and bowel infections and many others. However, cockroaches unlike mosquitoes do not transmit diseases directly to humans; they are merely pollutants and disease couriers or agents. Cockroaches feed on any plant and animal in their habitat. It is believed that cockroaches can go for days without food or water. It has been proved that cockroaches live for three months on water only.

Cockroaches are believed to have a long history of some medicinal benefits to humans besides being a delicacy. For example, cockroaches can be ground, boiled, or put in oil in some medicines for treatment of a variety of ailments. It is also believed that in the 1870's many New Orleanians in the United States of America had great faith in a remedy of boiled cockroach tea. It is also suggested that cockroaches help in the pollination of flowers in the tropical regions as they carry pollen from flowers as they move around. It is further agreed that cockroaches are invaluable agents in the re -cycling process as they scavenge the debris left by plants and animals. Cockroaches can also be used for medicinal testing. As a child I was not discouraged from eating food or milk infested with some dead cockroaches. I was advised to scoop out the dead cockroaches out, eat or drink my food. It was believed that eating such food was treatment for stomach, urinary, and headache ailments.Eating bugs is normal in many parts of the world, though the practice is taboo in the United States of America and many western countries.

Cockroach.

Cockroach (Bete): Boiled cockroaches were used in the treatment of certain ailments like stomachaches.
Photographer: Francisco Farias Jr.

Cockroach Recipes.

Jamaican Stir Fried Cockroaches.

Ingredients.
- 4 to 5 cockroaches (recently frozen)
- 1 onion
- 1 red pepper
- 1 green pepper
- 1 tablespoon salt
- 1 tablespoon starch
- 4 tablespoons cooking oil
- 2 cups rice

Instructions.
1. Remove and discard the solid wing covering flaps and all legs of the cockroach.
2. Put the whole cockroaches into a pot of boiling oil and quickly fry for 15 seconds.
3. Heat a wok until hot.
4. Add four spoons of oil and put all vegetables into it to stir fry for three minutes.
5. Put the half cooked cockroaches in to the wok and add salt and corn starch.
6. Serve on or with a bed of white rice.

Grubs/ Worms.

Red Palm Weevil.

The larval grub is considered a delicacy in much of Southeast Asia. "Sago Delight" or "Fried Sago Worms" are considered a delicacy in Malaysia, although versions of this dish can be found in many Southeast Asian countries and Papua New Guinea, where it is regarded as a delicacy. Sago grubs have been described as creamy tasting when raw, and like bacon or meat when cooked. They are often prepared with sago flour. In New Guinea, sago worms are roasted on a spit to celebrate special occasions. They are eaten either raw or roasted, and are regarded as a special high-nutrient meal. The taste of eating a live "butod" has been described as cheesy, rich and creamy. Some even said that it tasted far better than cream caramel. The worms are said to be clean enough to be eaten raw as they only live inside fallen sago tree trunks, feeding on the white sago pith.

Agave Worms.

Agave/ maguey worms can best be described as large fleshy caterpillars, rather than worms. They develop into a butterfly known as "mariposa". Agave worms are on the brink of extinction because of overharvesting for food and mescal. Most agave worms do not survive until adulthood to perpetuate the species. Agave/ maguey plants host caterpillars commonly called "agave worms."

Agave/ maguey worms are consumed in a wide variety of countries in South and Central America. They are even canned in Mexico to sell on the market, these plump critters have been said to taste something like sunflower seeds.

Agave Worms Recipe.

The agave worm is perfectly safe to eat. They are fried and eaten, "sans mescal", in Mexico, as part of a protein-rich diet. Some specialty markets even carried canned agave worms. Just add a spicy sauce and you have a nutritious snack.

Witchetty Grub.

This "cossid" moth, feeds on the roots of the Witchetty bush (named after the grubs) are found in central Australia. The term may also apply to larvae of other cossid moths, ghost moths, and longhorn beetles. The term is used mainly when the larvae are being considered as a delicacy. The grub is the most important insect food of the desert and was a staple in the diets of Aboriginal women. The different larvae are said to taste similar, probably because they have similar wood-eating habits. Witchetty grubs are edible either raw or lightly cooked in hot ashes, they are sought out as a high-protein food by indigenous Australians. The raw witchetty grub tastes like almonds and when cooked the skin becomes crisp like roast chicken while the inside becomes light yellow, like a fried egg.

Witchetty Grub Recipes.

WITCHETTY GRUB BARBECUE.

Matt Clark in the article," Insects are Food," said that 10 witchetty grubs are sufficient to provide the daily needs of an adult. The grub can be eaten raw, but if you wish you can cook them. The best way is to sear them all over in a hot pan until brown. You could try cooking them with some butter and even some garlic but he suggested that you keep it quite simple. The best way to eat them is to grab the head and just bite off the rest. You will find that the taste is quite pleasant having a fried egg flavor with a hint of nuts and the skin resembles that of fried chicken skin. The indigenous Australian folk have been eating witchetty grubs for years and regard them as a delicacy being good tasting and a great source of nutrition.

Witchetty Recipe.

TASTE OF THE OUTBACK: WITCHETTY GRUB.

Barbecued, witchetties are often eaten as an appetizer. They are cooked over a fire on pieces of wire, rather like shasliks or satays. It takes about two minutes each side for the meat to become white and chewy and the skin crusty. Barbecued witchetties taste quite like chicken or prawns with peanut sauce.

Fish.

Salmon.

Salmon. Lox is a Jewish delicacy that is usually
eaten on bagels with cream cheese.

Salmon and hake fillets are considered as delicacies in western
countries. There two types of hake namely silver and red hake.
Silver hake is also known as 'whiting' while the red hake is known as
'ling'. Hake is a member of the cod family though smaller. All hake
are deep – water fish that migrate inshore in warmer months. They
are mostly found in the eastern coast (Atlantic Ocean) of the United
States of America particularly around New York where they are
caught by commercial fishermen. Some of the hake fillet is exported
to the European Community Union countries. The prohibitive
cost of salmon has made it a delicacy in many cultures around the
world. Though salmon is readily available in abundance in some
countries like Canada, Japan and the United States of America
some salmon species like the white- king salmon or Ivory king are

considered a delicacy because of its scarcity. Ivory king salmon are highly valued, due in part to their scarcity in comparison to other Pacific salmon along most of the Pacific coast. Ivory kings make up only about 5 percent of the total salmon population. Lox is a Jewish smoked salmon that is considered a delicacy .It is usually eaten on bagels with cream cheese, but can be used in many other recipes. Once tossed aside as defective, this delicious fish has recently taken its rightful place at the head of the table and is one of the most sought-after of fine seafood.

There are at least six medicinal benefits derived from eating salmon meat and its products. These include; inflammation, cognitive function, and cancer prevention, eye health, cardiovascular health, and skin and hair health. There are 3 —mega fatty acids found in salmon fish which can be converted into some compounds which can prevent chronic inflammation. It has been proved scientifically that salmon intake is associated with decreased chances of depression, hostility in some teens, and a decreased cognitive decline in older people. Salmon meat and products are used in the treatment of a variety of cancers. Since salmon meat contains high levels of vitamin D and selenium which help in the prevention or decrease colorectal, prostate, and breast cancers.

Fish oil is good for improving vision. It has been proved that salmon products help in avoiding age related macular degeneration and chronic dry eye problems. Salmon products intake also decreases cardiovascular such as heart attack, stroke, and heart arrhythmia, and high blood pressure. Lastly, omega – 3 found in salmon lock moisture into skin cells encouraging the production of strong collagen elastic fibres which contribute to youthful looking skin and helps the nourishment to hair follicles which helps in prevention of hair loss. The high protein content in salmon fish also helps maintain strong, health hair.

Recipes.

Quick Salmon Chowder.

Ingredients.

    2 cups frozen pepper stir – fry
    2 cups tablespoon minced seeded jalapeno
    I teaspoon butter
    2 tablespoons flour
    2 cups fat – free half and half
    ½ teaspoon pepper
    Potatoes
    I -15 ounces salmon, drained and well flaked
    ¼ cup snipped watercress
    2 tablespoon lemon juice
    ½ teaspoon salt

Instructions.

1. In a large saucepan cook the stir-fry vegetables and jalapeno in hot margarine for 3 to 5 minutes or until tender.
2. Stir in flour.
3. Stir in milk and half and half.
4. Cook and stir until slightly thickened.
5. Cook and stir 2 minutes more.
6. Stir in potatoes, salmon, watercress, lemon juice, salt and pepper.
7. Cook and stir until heated through.

BBQ Salmon Salad.

Ingredients.

   2 tablespoons chili powder

   1 tablespoon garlic powder

   1 tablespoon onion powder

   3 tablespoons sugar

   ½ teaspoon ground cumin

   ¼ teaspoon ground white pepper

   1 tablespoon paprika

   6 (about 6 oz each) salmon fillets

   5 tablespoons olive oil

   1 ½ cups V8 100% vegetable oil juice

   1 tablespoon cider vinegar

   1 small tomato, chopped (about ½ cup)

   1 pound mixed salad greens

Instructions.

1. Stir the chili powder, garlic powder, onion powder, sugar, cumin, white pepper and paprika in a small bowl.
2. Reserve 1 1/2 tablespoons mixture for the dressing.
3. Sprinkle the salmon with the remaining seasoning mixture.
4. Cover the salmon and refrigerate for 6 hours.
5. Lightly oil the grill rack.
6. Heat the grill to high.
7. Brush the salmon with 1 tablespoon oil.
8. Grill for 8 minutes or until the salmon flakes easily when tested with a fork.
9. Beat the vegetable juice, vinegar, tomato, remaining oil and

reserved seasoning mixture in a large bowl with a fork or whisk until blended.

10. Add the salad greens and toss to coat.
11. Divide the salad among 6 plates.
12. Top with the salmon.

Kapenta Fish/ Matemba.

"Limnothrissa miodon" also known as Tanganyika Sardine. (Matemba)Kapenta is usually dried in the sun on a clean surface such as concrete slabs, rocks or netting.

Dried Kapenta Fish.

Kapenta fish is a small, freshwater sardine native to Lake Tanganyika in East Africa, (Tanzania, Uganda, and Kenya) which has been introduced to other lakes in Zambia, Zimbabwe and Mozambique. It is a staple source of protein in East Africa where it is sold in its dried form, however, kapenta fish can be sold in its fresh or frozen form. Canned kapenta fish is reserved for exports. Kapenta fish are caught at night using trawlers fitted with lights to attract them. Some Zimbabwean families do not have to buy the kapenta but use some traditional methods of catching fish such as hand gathering; angling and trapping. They risk their lives as they could be killed by crocodiles in the process. Crocodiles also feed on schools of kapenta.Some families in Zimbabwe are making a modest living through the sale of kapenta fish in Zimbabwe and Zambia. Kapenta fish is also popular with beer drinkers, who eat it as a snack. The kapenta fish population in Lake Kariba is threatened by overfishing by commercial fishermen and poaching because they have a ready market in cities and towns in Zambia and Zimbabwe. Kapenta fish population is also threatened by lates; these are large fish which feed on smaller fish for example the Nile Perch. Kapenta fish used to be cheap to buy but the price has spiked up making kapenta fish a delicacy in landlocked countries such as Zambia, Zimbabwe, and Botswana. It is believed that a cup of dried kapenta fish can feed a family.

A study done at Zambia's National Food and Nutrition Commission shows that kapenta fish is rich in protein, omega-3 and omega-6 fatty acids, vitamin B-12 and iron while low in saturated fat. Dried kapenta fish was also found to pack more calories and contain more iron and protein than fresh kapenta fish. There are several ways to cook kapenta fish. Kapenta fish can be dried and then cooked or it can be cooked fresh. Below are some ways to cook kapenta fish.

RECIPE.

Ingredients.

3 tablespoons of cooking oil

1 large onion

1 large tomato

1 pound of dried kapenta

Salt

Method.

1. Heat cooking oil in a pan over medium heat. Chop the onion and sauté the slices until they begin to turn brown.
2. Add slices of tomatoes and sauté for another two minutes.
3. Wash the dried kapenta fish under running water, and add to the ingredients in the pan. Cook five to seven minutes over high heat. Add 1/2 cup water, if you prefer wetter gravy for your kapenta stew. You can use peanut butter instead of cooking oil.

   If you are cooking fresh kapenta fish, add it after the sautéing the onion then add the slices of tomato after cooking for five minutes.

Source: Article reviewed by Kirk Ericson Last updated on: Sep 6, 2010

KAPENTA RECIPE.

Directions.

1. "Nshima/ Isitshwala/sadza": Requires starch powder (preferably maize meal). Mix contents with water and simmer for 10 minutes or so and then use a wooden spoon to thicken until hard.
2. Kapenta: This is tiny dried fish can be shallow fried with oil mixed with onions and tomatoes. The less spices the better not to mess with the original taste of the fish.
3. Beans: Can be white or red. Cook freestyle.
4. Rape: Green vegetables can be cooked whichever way you like e.g. cabbages, but best if shallow fried.

Lutefisk.

Lutefisk is a traditional dish of the Nordic countries. It is very popular in Nordic-North American areas of Canada. Lutefisk is made from aged stockfish air-dried whitefish or dried/salted whitefish also known as klippfisk and lye. It is gelatinous in texture, and has an extremely strong, pungent odor. Lutefisk is prepared with lye in a sequence of particular treatments. The watering steps of these treatments differ slightly for salted/dried whitefish because of its high salt content. The first treatment is to soak the stockfish in cold water for five to six days with the water changed daily. The saturated stockfish is then soaked in an unchanged solution of cold water and lye for an additional two days. The fish swells during this soaking, and its protein content decreases by more than 50 percent producing a jelly-like consistency. When this treatment is finished, the fish saturated with lye has an acid value of 11–12 and is therefore caustic. To make the fish edible, a final treatment of yet another four to six days of soaking in cold water also changed daily is needed. Eventually, the lutefisk is ready to be cooked.

There are several ways of cooking lutefisk for example, Lutefisk does not need additional water for the cooking; it is sufficient to place it in a pan, salt it, seal the lid tightly, and let it steam cook under a very low heat for 20–25 minutes. An alternative is to wrap in aluminum foil and bake at 225 °C (435 °F) for 40–50 minutes. You can also boil Lutefisk directly in a pan of water. Fill the pan 2/3 full with water, add 2 teaspoons of salt per liter water, and bring the water to a boil. Add lutefisk pieces to the water until they all are covered with water, and let it simmer for 7 to 8 minutes. Carefully lift the lutefisk out of the water and serve.

It is important to clean the lutefisk and its residue off pans, plates, and utensils immediately. Lutefisk left overnight becomes nearly impossible to remove. Sterling silver should never be used in the cooking, serving or eating of lutefisk, which will permanently ruin silver. Stainless steel utensils are recommended instead.

Bugs.

Stink Bug.

STINK BUGS ARE GENERALLY found in the warmer parts of the world for example in Africa. They are mostly found in southern Africa in countries such as Botswana, South Africa, and Zimbabwe, Mozambique, Zambia and Venda. The name stink bug is derived from the pungent smell they produce as a defensive mechanism when they are threatened or attacked. The pungent smell comes from the glands located on the dorsal surface of the abdomen and the underside of the thorax. Humans eat them as a delicacy or part of their culture. The stink bug also known as (harugwa) by the locals is not found everywhere in Zimbabwe but in isolated areas particularly between Masvingo and Zaka. Some families make a living through the sale of these bugs in winter. Stink-bug is used in some cultures to add flavor to stews or as a snack. Those who sampled the stink bugs say that they have a bitter taste.

The Venda people in South Africa eat stink bugs as part of their diet although they sell some of the stink bugs. The edible stink-bug is known in Venda as 'thongolifha'. Unlike the Mopani worm, or Mashonzha, which hibernate underground in the pupa stage before turning into the Mopani emperor moth, "thongolifha" hibernates in the adult stage and never go underground. This means that the fully grown 'thongolifha' can be harvested in winter when there is little other food available. Women and children usually collect stink bugs early in the morning when they cannot fly because it will be cold. Stink bug harvesters usually use their hands, however, some wear some plastic bags which act as gloves to protect themselves from the defensive secretions which cause some orange stains on their hands or eye irritation. The stink bug is a herbivore feeding on leaves, fruits and vegetables. Below are some suggested ways of preparing stink bugs for family consumption and for sale:

Separate dead bugs and debris from live bugs. Place the live bugs in bucket with some warm water and stir with a wooden stick (mugoti) to remove the pungent scent. Be warned that there will be a very strong smell from the defensive secretions which cause eye irritation. Add some more warm water and rinse the stink bugs. Repeat this process three times. Boil the stink bugs for a while and then sun dry the stink bugs on plastics or empty corn jute bags. Grade the stink bugs according to size and quality and pack them in bags for sale or family consumption.

Giant Water Bug.

Giant water bugs are related to water scorpions, assassin bugs, stink bugs, and many more. They can swim and fly. They have evolved from herbivores to carnivores as they can suck blood and body fluid from their prey. The giant water bug is believed to be a native of Japan. However, giant water bugs are considered a delicacy in China where they are nicknamed toe biters because they can inflict a deadly painful stab with their front beak. Giant water bugs are also found in some East Asian countries such as Thailand, Indonesia, Vietnam and others. Giant water bugs are generally found in such places as stagnant or slowly moving water, particularly where there is emergent vegetation. Giant water bugs have developed some hunting techniques for example, ambushing their prey such as small fish, frogs, and snakes. They can grab hold of a plant near the surface, and stick their short breathing tube out of the water to allow them to breathe while waiting for their prey.They use their powerful front legs to grab their prey and inject some venom which kills or paralyses their prey. They pierce their prey with their sharp beak and secrete digestive enzymes that dissolve the body tissues and then suck out the liquefied remains. Giant water bugs are often collected using large floating traps on ponds, set with black lights to attract the bugs.

Giant Water Bug Recipe.

Giant water bugs are either sautéed or fried in oil, garlic, onions and tomatoes, or roasted, after the wings and legs have been removed, and eaten as a viand for steamed rice or as a finger food with liquor in the Philippines.

Giant Water Scorpions.

Water scorpions are considered a delicacy in East Asia particularly in Thailand cuisine where they are used mainly for their special aroma. They can also be barbecued and served as a snack. Water scorpions are aquatic insects that are found all over the world.They are commonly called water scorpions because of their superficial resemblance to scorpions, which is due to their raptorial forelegs and the presence of a long slender process at the posterior end of the abdomen, resembling a tail. Water scorpions are dark brown or blackish-brown in color. They are flying insects with well-developed wings; however, they prefer to walk in the mud or between aquatic plants. They are poor swimmers. Water scorpions are carnivores and feed on small fish, tadpoles and other aquatic insects. The most interesting feature is their feeding habit. It has been observed that they hang still with their body upside down, until the prey is within their grasp. Another added advantage is that their excellent camouflage, which makes them inconspicuous to their prey. Once a prey approaches, a water scorpion seizes it with its hind legs. It then injects a digestive enzyme in the prey and sucks out the body fluids, leaving behind an empty shell.

The water scorpion's sting is very painful though not poisonous as that of a land scorpion. It has been observed that the water scorpions have a variety of breeding systems. Water scorpions breed once annually and the breeding is in spring. They lay their eggs among leaf debris or in the stem of aquatic vegetation. However, some water scorpion species lay their eggs on the back of the male water scorpion. During this breeding process, the female secretes waterproof glue that helps in fixing the eggs. The male then looks after the eggs, till they hatch. Like most insects ,water scorpions do not look after their young ones. The young ones fend for themselves putting at the mercy of some predators.

WATER SCORPION RECIPE.

Ingredients.
   ½ cup vegetable oil
   30 -40 live water scorpions
   125 g fresh pork
   1 large garlic bulb, crushed
   Fresh ginger root, about 3 cm, chopped
   Salt
   ½ liter water
   1 handful dried Chinese dates
   1 handful dried red berries
   1 large carrot, sliced
   Pepper to taste.

Directions.
1. Heat the oil in a large wok.
2. Stir-fry the scorpions for 20 seconds.
3. Add the pork, garlic, salt and pepper. Stir-fry briefly,
4. Add the water slowly.
5. Add the other ingredients and simmer on a low heat for 40 minutes.

The Mole Cricket.

Mole crickets look like moles hence they got their name. Mole crickets vary in size and appearance, but most of them are of moderate size. They are muscular, the abdomen is rather soft, but the head, forelimbs, and thorax are heavily hardened. The hind legs are shaped somewhat like the legs of any other cricket, but are more adapted for shoving while digging. They are mostly nocturnal insects and forage on plants root system causing a lot of damage to lawn turfs, irrigation ditches such as sugar plantations, and vegetables potatoes, and wheat fields as they tunnel underground. They also feed grubs and earthworms.

Some mole crickets are very good fliers as they can fly up to five miles during mating seasons. Mole crickets are known as "ndororo" in some parts of Zimbabwe while the Philippines call them "kamaro". They are mostly found in some wetlands known as "mapani". However, it is rare to find mole crickets in Zimbabwe because of climate change, the water table in most wetlands has gone down; humans have also turned such areas farmlands. Mole crickets can only be found near river and dam banks or in lawns. Some people speculate that the mole cricket is the ugliest of all crickets. I am not sure what their standard measurement is. Mole crickets are also found in the southeast and southwest of the United States of America, for example in Florida and Texas.

The mole cricket is a much sought after delicacy in the Philippines. The Philippines have developed several recipes and themes of preparing and cooking the mole cricket. Below are some of the mole cricket themes I have selected.

Some people like to stir-fry them without any oil or flavoring, preferring a taste they give off that way, slightly like liver. Once cooked, you can eat them totally but most folks prefer to take off claws, legs and wings.

The next cooking method is cooking them in oil with garlic, onions and vinegar. Some mole cricket consumers like to flavor them with soy sauce and vinegar. To make the classic dish of "Kamaro," boil them in vinegar and garlic. Drain, remove the legs, wings, claws and then sauté the bodies in oil, chopped onion and tomatoes until they are chocolate brown. They go very well with cold beer. They are crispy on the outside, moist in the middle. If you like a scratchy texture, leave the wings, legs and claws on.

The last common recipe takes a slightly different approach. Numb them, remove the scratchy parts, then sauté in garlic and onions with soy sauce, vinegar and hot pepper. You may add coconut milk to thicken the sauce.

Offal.

SOME CULTURES SHY AWAY from offal as food, particularly the United States of America, while others use it as everyday food, or as delicacies. Offal refers to the internal organs and entrails of slaughtered mammals, reptiles, and birds. Offal may include may include such organs as the stomach, intestines, and liver, blood, and pancreas, fat, heart, and lungs, trachea, and tongue, kidney, and eyes. Birds' feet, bones, and their heads are also known as offal. Offal has different names depending on the country, culture and parts consumed. For example, haggis, faggots, "kaszanka" in Scotland, Middle England, and Poland respectively. In some Latin American countries, such as Mexico, almost all internal parts and organs are consumed regularly. Chicken hearts, gizzards and livers are usually eaten fried or boiled, either alone, or in broth. However, some cultures chose to eat some parts of the offal or some parts of the offal are reserved for a particular gender and age. For example:

In the Kikuyu traditions, grilled goat/sheep kidneys are a delicacy usually reserved for young ladies, similarly, the tongue was reserved for men and the ears were to be eaten by little girls. The testicles were for the young men. Liver is also consumed by all members of the family. The heads, lungs and hooves of animals are boiled to make soup and sometimes mixed with herbs for medicinal purposes. Offal dishes in South Africa do not usually consist of any organs and are mostly limited to stomach, skin, sheep's head, shin and very rarely brains.

In Zimbabwe offal is a common relish and delicacy enjoyed by people of all tribes and cultures. Offal was mostly consumed by the poor, because it was cheap to buy. However, the middle class males nowadays consumed a lot of offal at beer parties, particularly the intestines, liver, pancreas, and the trachea. They normally roast "braai" the offal. Some women in Zimbabwe make a good living out of roasting offal and other beef cuts at beer outlets in some high density suburbs which they serve with some salads. Zimbabweans call the beef and chicken offal binge "gotchi –gotchi" from the Shona word "gocha" which means roasting. Cow, goat, and sheep offal dishes include stomach, hooves, shin, intestines, liver, head, tongue and very rarely in certain communities, testicles and a bull's penis. Chicken dishes include feet, liver, and intestines, gizzards, heads, and hearts. Married men occasionally mix cow feet with herbs as an aphrodisiac. They carry the "aphrodisiac" exercise away from their wives and usually in groups of friends. They cook the cow's feet while drinking beer or may be playing social soccer. I have eaten both the bull's testicles and a cow's udder. I am yet to taste a bull's penis but my friends told me that it tastes like rubber or a ligament. Women and girls are strictly prohibited from eating a bull's testicles, penis and udder. I do not know the reason either spiritually or culturally. No one has given me a good reason for the prohibition.

A popular preparation for goat or sheep offal involves wrapping pieces of the manageable pieces of stomach with the intestines before cooking. Zimbabweans do not bleach the stomach or gut of any domesticated animal. They only wash the dung in the gut using plain water and then cut the gut into manageable pieces and cook it in clay pots over an open fire. More often they mix the gut with cow intestines, lungs, and some raw fat from the animal and cook them together. The end result is a tasty meal. I have personally eaten such a meal. Zimbabweans believe that over washing the gut takes away the "gut" flavor. The eating of cow feet, gut, heart, and pancreas, liver and intestines except those three organs I have alluded to above, is family friendly as there are no restrictions on who eats cow gut. I have never seen Zimbabweans eat animal eyes. I have observed some Zimbabweans preparing and cooking animal skins particularly goat skin.

Pig Brain.

Some cultures find the eating of any animal brain as offensive or distasteful. Some people use animal brain as nourishment to other foods. There are several myths and scientific theories about the advantages of eating pig brain or any other animal brain. Some western cultures are refraining from eating cow brain because of the mad cow disease prevalence. Animal rights activists preach against the eating of animal brain because of the cruelty and graphic methods these animals are killed in order to extract the brain. For example it is suggested that a captured monkey may be pulled to a dining table where it is held with hoops over its legs and hands. It is suggested that one of the dinners uses a hammer to knock out the monkey's head to open a hole large enough for the dinners to use a stick of iron rod to extract the monkey's brain. The monkey may scream but no avail.

Some people speculate that the brain of a pig has a very "rich" taste while others say it is horrible. The brain of a pig is also high in cholesterol just like the brain of any animal. Some scientists speculate that since the pig or any other animal brain contains complex carbohydrates, proteins, and omega – 3 fatty acids, iron, and antioxidants you can improve your concentration, memory, and blood circulation, alertness, and slow the aging process. Some Zimbabweans eat pig brain because of these assertions. However, most Zimbabweans perceive that eating pig brain is offensive and distasteful.

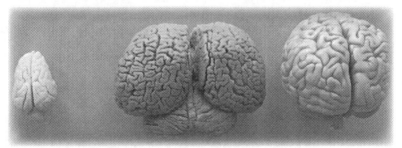

Pig Brain: Some people believe that eating pig brain enhances human memory or life longevity.

Pig Brain Recipes.

1. Poach the pig's brain very gently in a traditional court bouillon for about 5 minutes. Then the membrane is removed and it is ready to be taken to the next step towards a finished dish.
2. In a sauté pan over medium heat add a nug of butter and let it brown place the seasoned poached brain in the pan presentation side down.
3. Add the sliced porcinis and place in the oven for 3 minutes remove from the over an flip the brain over and add the capers.
4. Deglaze the pan with lemon juice and a splash of chicken stock, add a bit of butter and let the sauce reduce finish with parsley and serve.

Egg and Pig Brain.

Ingredients.

2 ½ tablespoons

4 eggs

1/3 cup of whole milk

¼ teaspoon freshly ground black pepper

¼ teaspoon salt

1 can (5 ounces) pork brains in gravy (Rose Brand preferred)

Instructions.

1. Melt bacon grease in an iron skillet on low heat.
2. Add pork brains to heated grease.
3. Stir with a fork.
4. Add salt and pepper and stir.
5. Whisk eggs and milk together.
6. Increase heat and add egg mixture to brains.
7. Scramble to desired consistency.
8. Serve immediately over toast.
9. For a truly southern dish, serve with grits and apple butter.

Offal: Offal can be a cheaper type of food .

Most Americans cringe at the thought or sight of eating the foot of any animal, but in many cultures, cow feet are used for flavoring ingredients to soups and stew or are consumed as inexpensive sources of meat. A cow's foot does not have a great deal of tender meat, but when it is slowly simmered the tough fibers of the foot soften and the meat can be removed from the bone. Enjoy it with the broth as a soup or eaten as is. Some men in Zimbabwe put some aphrodisiac herbs when the cow feet are ready for consumption. Cow feet are a favorite with beer imbibers. Women supplement their family incomes by selling these prepared cow feet. However, some eat cow feet at the family dining table. Cow feet are a delicacy in some different parts of the world such as many parts of Africa, Jamaica, China, Mexico and many others.

Cow Foot recipes.

Cow Foot Stew.

1. Place the cow's foot, onion, garlic, salt, pepper and water into a large saucepan. Bring the water to a boil over high heat.

2. Reduce the heat to medium-low and simmer the cow's foot for three hours, uncovered. At the end of the cooking time, the cooking broth should be reduced to 4 or 5 cups and the meat on the cow's foot should be tender and falling off the bone.

3. Remove the cow's foot from the stockpot with tongs. Remove the meat from the bone and discard the bone. Set the meat aside.

4. Strain the broth into another large saucepan and discard the solids. Heat the broth over high heat until it boils then reduces the heat to medium and whisk in the flour. Simmer the broth, whisking constantly, until it is reduces and thickened to your desired consistency.

5. Serve the hot gravy over the cow's foot.

Cow Foot Soup

Ingredients

    1 medium cow foot

    1 large carrot (chopped)

    2 Irish potatoes

    8 – 10 spice seeds

    1 teaspoon (5ml) salt

    ¼ lb macaroni (broken into small pieces)

    1 onion (sliced)

    2 plugs garlic (crushed)

    1 can vegetable soup (optional)

    ½ teaspoon (2ml) black pepper

    ½ (2ml) thyme

    ½ - lb tripe (optional)

Directions.

Preparing Cow.

1.   Clean cow foot well.
2.   Boil for about 45 minutes and throw off the water (to make less sticky).

Method

1.   Add freshwater and spice seeds. Boil with tripe until tender. (Use a pressure cooker if available).
2.   Add potatoes, carrots, macaroni, onion and garlic.
3.   Season to taste with salt, pepper and thyme
4.   Add soup.
5.   Cook for about 3 – 5 minutes more.
6.   Serve hot

Zimbabwean Recipe.

The cow head is properly cleaned and burnt to remove the hair from the skin. The head can also be clean-shaven with a razor and then burnt, while others prefer to skin the cow head or fragment it using an ax and the desired parts of the head are restored for cooking. The brain, eyes, ears and tongue are cooked are traditionally in a heavy mortar, with onion, garlic and ginger paste, lots of tomatoes, chilies and other seasonings. The dish is traditionally eaten with fingers. Rural Zimbabweans, especially among the Shona reserve the cow head for the father as head of the family. The head is normally prepared by sons-in law at some traditional ceremonies. They risk a fine if they do not meet the required traditional cooking standards.

How to Prepare a Cow Head.

1. Procure skinned cows' heads from a slaughterhouse. The heads must be intact, containing the teeth, eyes, tongue and brain. These heads are inevitably filthy, and must be thoroughly cleaned.
2. Attach a pressure nozzle to the hose. Spray each cow's head thoroughly inside and out. The hose and nozzle is usually inserted through the neck opening to rinse out blood and mucous.
3. Wrap the cows' heads in several layers of heavy-duty aluminum foil. The heads must be completely covered, with no cracks or gaps apparent. Set the heads aside.
4. Fill the firebox of the smoker with a large amount of charcoal briquettes. Light the briquettes, and allow them to burn to a white-hot, smoldering state. While the coals are burning, pour hickory chips into a bucket of water. Allow them to soak for a minimum of 30 minutes.

5. Spread the hickory chips over the white-hot coals. Allow the smoker to reach 225 degrees Fahrenheit. Place the wrapped cows' heads on the smoker's cooking grate.

6. Continue to add charcoal to the firebox over the next 12 to 24 hours; keep the smoker's temperature at between 225 and 250 degrees Fahrenheit. Allow a minimum of one hour of cooking time per lb. A 20-lb. cow's head must cook for at least 20 hours.

7. Remove the heads from the smoker, and tear off the foil. Separate the meat from the heads with your fingers, and place it in separate pans. Dedicate one pan for the cheek meat and tongue, one for the brains and eyes and one for various pieces of meat found on and in the head

Smoked Cow Head Barbacoa.

Ingredients.
  1 cow head
  Salt, pepper and cayenne
  2 bottles of beer
  Long banana leaves

Method:
1. Sprinkle the salt, pepper and cayenne all over the cow head
2. Completely wrap the cow head in several layers of banana leaves, securing it with kitchen twine.
3. In a banana-leaf-lined hotel pan, pour two bottles of beer.
4. Set the banana-leaf-wrapped cow head into the pan, and fold over pan-lining leaves.
5. Cover cow head and bottom pan with another hotel pan.
6. Secure tight with kitchen twine.
7. Smoke for 24 hours, remove meat from head (will have to peel the skin off of the tongue), pull apart and make tacos!

Source: Elizabeth Karmel.

Barbacoa de Cabeza

In the Rio Grande Valley, barbacoa de Cabeza is traditionally eaten on Sunday mornings.

Ingredients.
1 Cabeza, beef head
4 large Texas yellow onions
3 heads garlic
2 bunches of cilantro
Salt to taste.
Pepper Corn or flour tortillas
Pico de gallo and your favorite salsa(s)

Directions.
1. Before you actually get the Cabeza (beef head), understand that it won't look very nice -in fact it will look pretty gruesome. Therefore, I suggest purchasing the head the day you cook it.
2. Clean the Cabeza, removing eyes, ears, etc. Discard the tongue. Leaving it will impart an odd taste to the meat. Sprinkle salt and pepper over the whole Cabeza. Wrap the Cabeza in a paper sack, along with onions, garlic, and cilantro. Wrap THAT in burlap.
3. Dig a hole 2 feet deep and build a driftwood fire in it. Wait until the fire goes to coals, and then cover them with ashes, followed by the Cabeza, then about 2 inches of dry dirt or sand. Fill up the hole. Add 6 to 8 inches of dirt or sand over it. Build a fire on top of the ground. Use slow-burning wood such as oak or mesquite.
4. Leave the Cabeza in the whole 12 to 18 hours. For

example, if you begin cooking it at 4:00 p.m., it should be ready by the next morning. Serve with tortillas. If your spouse objects to the digging the hole in the backyard, then wrap the Cabeza in foil and bake it in an oven or over a charcoal grill. Using foil in place of the paper bag keeps the Cabeza slightly moister while it is cooking. I also suggest not 'cleaning' the head in the kitchen-tends to strain a marriage.

Source: Shin.

Tripe. (Matumbhu/Guru).

Tripe may make someone's stomachs turn, but many ethnicities treasure it. Tripe is the lining of the first three stomachs (guru) of ruminants (cattle, sheep, goats) etc. Tripe includes the rumen (blanket/flat/smooth tripe), the reticulum (honeycomb and pocket tripe) the omasum (book, bible, leaf (Susu /tsitsa) tripe), and the abomasums (reed).Tripe can also be produced from any animal with a stomach for example the pig's paunch. Tripe can be categorized as unwashed (green) and washed tripe. Unwashed tripe includes some of the stomach's last contents. It emits some foul smell which makes it undesirable to eat. Some developed countries use tripe as pet food. Washed tripe is also referred to as dressed tripe. It is cleaned and the fat trimmed. It is then boiled and bleached giving it the white color more commonly associated with tripe we see in most butchery. It needs a professional butcher to wash and clean the tripe.

How some Zimbabweans Prepare Tripe.

The cleaning of tripe (guru) the intestines (matumbhu) using water is usually done by women. Daughters-in-law clean tripe at traditional ceremonies. After cleaning the tripe they cut it into manageable pieces for cooking. They cook the tripe in a stockpot or clay pot on an open fire for about two to three hours. They add tomatoes, onion and salt when the tripe is cooked.

Beef intestines are used as casings for sausages in some cultures, but quite often the intestines and the stomach, or tripe, are cooked for use in a number of dishes, such as soups and stews. It has been observed that cooking the intestines slowly produces a flavorful broth and a meat with a soft, chewy texture.

Tripe Recipes.

BOILED TRIPE.
1. Clean the beef intestines, or tripe, under cold running water.
2. Flatten the tripe with your hand and cut it into 1-inch-square pieces with a sharp knife. Make sure you use a combination of honeycomb tripe and smooth blanket tripe from the cow.
3. Place the chopped tripe in a large stockpot filled with water.
4. Place garlic cloves, peppercorns, thyme and bay leaves into a piece of cheesecloth. Tie the cheesecloth closed, creating a small bundle of spices.
5. Drop the bundle into the water. Bring the pot to a boil over medium-high heat, skimming any foam that might rise to the top of the water with a serving spoon.

6. Turn the heat to low. Allow the pot to simmer for 2 to 3 hours, or until the tripe becomes tender.
7. Add canned hominy, salt, chopped cilantro and chopped green onions to the stock pot.
8. Allow the tripe to cook for an additional 15 to 20 minutes.
9. Remove the bundle of spices and serve.

Sautéed Tripe.

1. Place whole beef intestines, or tripe, into a large stockpot.
2. Cover the tripe with water, at least 2 inches above the tripe.
3. Add vanilla and vinegar to the water.
4. Bring the tripe to a boil over high heat.
5. Turn the heat to low and simmer the tripe between 1 hour and 1-1/2 hours.
6. Drain the water from the tripe and allow it to cool.
7. Use a sharp knife to slice the tripe into 1-inch pieces.
8. Heat olive oil on high in a large skillet.
9. Add sliced red onions, chopped garlic and the sliced tripe to the hot oil.
10. Sauté the tripe in the skillet for 3 to 4 minutes, or until the onions become translucent.
11. Add tomato sauce to the tripe. Bring the tripe and tomato sauce to boil.
12. Turn the heat to low and simmer covered for about 30 minutes

Source. Cecilia Harsch.

Eating of beef intestines known as 'gopchang' is part of Korea's culture and history. It was believed that eating of beef intestines would give strength and stamina to the weak and the sick. It also had some medicinal properties. It is further suggested that eating beef intestines helped prevent diabetes and was good for the skin. However, beef intestines contain a large amount of protein and enzymes which create a bad smell. It is recommended that in order to remove the bad smell and blood, the intestines should be soaked in water. After being soaked, the intestines are often marinated in garlic and ginger. History has it that Koreans did not eat lots of intestines before the time of Japan's colonization. The Japanese took every good beef cuts except the intestines. The Koreans resorted to eating intestines, which caught the Japanese by surprise. The Japanese thought the Koreans were savage, but they actually liked eating beef intestines after they tried it. Since then, beef intestines have become a delicacy both in Korea and Japan, but Japanese eat more ox tripe than intestines.

Goat Gut Recipe.

GOAT GUT.

1. Turn the goat intestines inside out, and clean them thoroughly in a bowl of water. Scrape off the sticky dirt with a knife.
2. Cut up the other goat entrails into smaller pieces and wash them. Drain them in a colander, and transfer them into a clean bowl.
3. Sprinkle the salt, cheese, pepper and oregano on the cleaned lamb entrails. Spread 1 tsp. of olive oil on the seasoned entrails.
4. Put the pieces of the entrails on the skewer, mixing pieces

of liver, lungs, heart and kidneys. Drape the thin fat membrane over the rest of the entrails.

5. Wrap the goat intestine over the fat membrane. Stand the skewer upright for 10 minutes to let the juices drip. Mix the lemon juice with the rest of the olive oil.

6. Cook the goat intestines over low heat on a spit for 3 hours, basting regularly with the mixture of lemon juice and olive oil.

How to prepare Goat Gut.

Choose a thick cut of tripe if buying raw. The muscular stomach tissue should be white in color.

1. Find fresh tripe or purchase packaged tripe from grocery store. Cooking fresh tripe is more involved. Packaged tripe has usually been cooked for a bit to soften it up for preparing.

2. Wash the tripe multiple times to rid it of particles of food or other pieces of matter. It may take three to four vigorous washings before the tripe is ready to be cooked.

3. Boil the tripe for at least four to five hours in a clay pot or stockpot of water. Tripe is a notoriously tough food. The longer you boil it, the tenderer it becomes.

4. Cut the tender, boiled tripe into pieces. Sauté the pieces in butter; add seasonings and sauce and simmer for at least one hour.

Animal Eyes, Ears, and Tongues.

Sheep eyes are considered a delicacy in some world cultures. In some parts of Arabia, sheep's eyes are given to the guest of honor at the table. It is customary that ear and eye are eaten first, because they are the fattiest areas and are best eaten warm. In some cultures, stuffed cow's eyes are considered a delicacy. They are made by first removing the vitreous humor, lens, cornea, and iris, and then boiled. Cow eyes are often stuffed with varieties of coleslaw, beef, and even cream cheese. The Inuit believe that seal eyes are a source of zinc in their diet. The sheep's head or lamb is considered a delicacy in Norway where it is known as "smalahovud", and the eyes are also eaten.

Tongue and tongue parts are considered delicacies in some cultures around the world.Tounge is prepared in different ways for example, hot tongue sandwiches are found on menus in kosher delicatessens in America, taco "de lengua"in Mexican cuisine. , tongue in sauce in Colombian gastronomy, is a dish prepared by frying the tongue, adding tomato sauce, onions and salt. Duck tongues are sometimes used in Szechuan dishes, while lamb's tongue is occasionally used in Continental and contemporary American cooking. Fried cod "tongue" is a relatively common part of fish meals in Norway and Newfoundland. In Argentina and Uruguay cow tongue is cooked and served in vinegar while the Czech Republic and Poland consider a pork tongue as a delicacy. Beef and pork tongues fetch significantly higher prices and are considered more of delicacy in Eastern Slavic countries. Pork and beef tongues are commonly consumed, boiled and garnished with horseradish or jelled.

Pig Eyes.

Pig Eyes (Maziso): Pig's eyes are the fattiest areas of pork and are best eaten warm. In some cultures the eyes of certain animals are eaten, though it is not widely practiced. Some of the most common animal eyes eaten include sheep and fish eyes.

Recipes.

How to Cook Fish Eyes.

Ingredients.
Fish eye balls
Onion, chopped
Lemongrass
Coconut, chopped
Tomato, diced
Ginger
Fish chunks
Sweet potato
Salt to taste
Vegetable oil/ butter

Directions.
1. Melt the vegetable oil in a sauce pan on medium heat.
2. Sauté the onion, lemongrass and ginger until the onion turns translucent. Use butter if you prefer, though vegetable oil is lower in saturated fat and cholesterol.
3. Add the sweet potato and stir to coat it with the oil mixture.
4. Wear gloves to avoid getting fish eye liquids on your hands. Squeeze the fish eyeballs to release the liquid contents into the soup and stir the liquids together.
5. Discard the solid pieces because they do not add to the texture or flavor of the soup.

6. Pour in the vegetable broth and coconut milk. Use low sodium broth and light coconut milk to reduce calories and salt. Simmer for 20 minutes, or until the potatoes soften.
7. Add the fish chunks and tomato. Simmer for additional 10 minutes.

Remove the lemongrass and serve.

Source: Kristin Dorman.

How to Smoke Beef Tongue.

You Need.
  Beef tongue
  Vegetable brush
  Stockpot
  ¼ cup salt
  2 tablespoons of garlic, chopped
  1 bottle of beer
  2 tablespoons of black pepper
  2 green onions
  Sharp kitchen knife
  Smoker
  Pecan wood
  Apple wood
  Meat thermometer

Instructions.
1. Wash the beef tongue under cold water with a stiff vegetable brush.
2. Place the tongue in a large stockpot and fill the pot with cold water. The tongue should be covered by 2 to 3 inches of water.
3. Add 1/4 cup of salt to the water.
4. Soak beef tongue for one hour in the refrigerator.
5. Replace salted water in the stockpot with fresh, cold water. Soak tongue for one more hour in the refrigerator. If the water clouds up during this time, replace it.
6. Drain water from pot. Pour one bottle of beer into the pot

with the tongue. Add enough cold water to the pot to cover the tongue by 2 to 3 inches.

7. Add 2 tbsp. of chopped garlic, 2 tsp. of black pepper and two chopped green onions to the pot.

8. Simmer the tongue in this mixture for one hour with the pot covered.

9. Remove the tongue from the pot and run cold water over it until it is cool to the touch. Peel the skin off the tongue with a sharp kitchen knife and remove any excess fat.

10. Set smoker, filled with pecan and apple wood, to 200 degrees. Smoke tongue for four hours.

11. Check the temperature of the tongue with a meat thermometer. The internal temperature should be 175 degrees. If it has not reached this temperature, cook the meat longer.

12. Remove the tongue from the smoker and allow it to cool.

Source: Audra Dean, eHow Contributor.

BEEF TONGUE.

Ingredients.
 Beef tongue
 1 large onion sliced
 1 carrot grated
 8 Allspice berries
 1 teaspoon black pepper peppercorns
 5 cloves
 A bay leaf
 3 -4 cloves of garlic
 Salt to taste

Instructions.
1. Scrub the tongue very well and put in a huge pot with cold water to just cover.
2. Add an onion, sliced or not, a carrot, grated, 8 allspice berries, 1 tsp. black peppercorns, 5 cloves, a bay leaf, 3-4 cloves of garlic, and some salt.
3. Simmer for about 3 hours, keeping the tongue just barely covered.
4. Remove from stock and let cool, just a bit! The skin of the tongue on the taste bud side will have pulled away a bit from the meat.
5. Slit this with a sharp knife, don't hit the meat. Scissors work well. Then just peel off both sides.
6. 6. Cut the root end off and freeze for a soup. It has a lot of gnarly things in it, but makes a good little soup when picked apart.

7. Slice the tongue and put into an oven dish with a ladle-full of the stock.
8. Cover and keep warm in the oven.
9. Strain the stock, pressing hard on the solids.
10. Bring to a boil and reduce to 2-3 cups.
11. Taste for seasoning and thicken with a cornstarch paste.
12. Pour the liquid in the baking dish into the gravy and whisk it in.
13. Pour over the meat.

Beef Liver with Onions.

Ingredients.
- ¼ cup soy sauce
- 1 teaspoon granulated sugar
- 1 teaspoon chicken soup base or bouillon granules
- 1 pound beef liver
- 2 tablespoons vegetable oil
- 1 large onion, halved

Directions.
1. Combine soy sauce, sugar and chicken soup base in medium bowl.
2. Add liver; stir to coat.
3. Cover; marinate in refrigerator, stirring occasionally, for 30 minutes.
4. Heat vegetable oil in large skillet over medium-high heat.
5. Add onions; cook, stirring frequently, for 5 to 6 minutes or until golden.
6. Place liver over onions; cook on each side for 3 to 4 minutes or until no longer pink in center

Animal Testicles.

Many people would grimace or cringe at the idea of eating the testicles of an animal. I have eaten a bull's, hog's tecticles and a cow's udder but I shudder to eat a bull's penis and anus, however, they are considered a delicacy, an aphrodisiac in some cultures around the world. Some cultures have created festivals to celebrate, prepare and feasts on the coveted meat known as the testes.For example Serbia hosted the "The Ball Cup Championship" which attracted world renowned chefs from Canada, Australia, and United States of America, United Kingdom, New Zealand, and China, Japan and many others. The chefs competed in cooking bull, wild boar, and kangaroo, donkey, and horse, reindeer, ostrich and turkey testicles and many more. The Fear Food Festival was held in New Zealand where the deer penis and ox tongue featured at the festival. The festival also attracted some chefs all over the world and competed in the cooking of deer penis and ox tongue among other dishes. Depending on where you live, eating balls may not be that uncommon. You can find them on menus in regions big on cattle ranching including Texas and in farming areas throughout North America.

You have to be careful on what you order in American restaurants and hotels. In the United States they call testicles by different names such as rocky mountain oysters or mountain oysters, prairie oysters, hog balls, calf fries and turkey testicles. They cook and serve them battered, breaded, deep fried and pan fried, as appetizers and main course dishes as well as sliced and fried and made into a sandwich and enjoyed with a number of toppings similar to a "po' boy". Some people say that the meat of the mountain oyster is as tender as the loin and tastes just as good or better. It is a fact that eating bulls' testicles is an acquired taste.

Testicles Recipes.

CALF/BULL FRIES RECIPE.

Ingredients.
- 2 pounds calf or bull testicles
- 2 cups beer
- 2 eggs, beaten
- 2 eggs, beaten
- 1 ½ cups all purpose flour
- Salt and ground black pepper to taste
- Vegetable oil
- ¼ cup yellow cornmeal
- 1 tablespoon hot pepper sauce

Directions.
1. Use enough vegetable oil to fill your frying container halfway to the top (to allow for bubbling up and splattering) and to completely cover calf testicles while frying.
2. With a very sharp knife, split the tough skin-like muscle that surrounds each testicle.
3. Remove the skin (you can remove the skin easily if the testicles are frozen, then peel while thawing).
4. Slice each testicle into approximately ¼- to ½- inch-thick ovals.
5. Place slices in a large pan or blow with enough beer to cover them; cover and let sit 2 hours.
6. In a shallow bowl, combine eggs, flour, cornmeal, salt, and pepper.

7. Remove testicles from beer; drain and dredge thoroughly in the flour mixture.
8. In a large, deep pot, heat oil to 375° F. Deep fry 3 to 4 minutes or until golden brown (will rise to the surface when done).
9. Drain on paper towels.

Recipe.

Fish Intestines.

Fish Tripe Soup.

Ingredients.
 250 g oil – frying – expanded dried fish tripe
 Chicken mousse
 Egg white
 Tomato
 Green cabbage hearts Gourmet powder and water
 chestnut powder
 Chives
 Dried scallops
 Shrimp meat
 Peas
 Cucumber
 Peanuts
 Black moss
 Salt Ginger Pepper
 Rice wine
 Salad oil

Instructions.
1. Coat the shrimp meat with seasoning paste,
2. Move it in the heated oil in a frying pot to be done, and then drain off oil.
3. Steam the dried scallops and peanuts to be well-done,
4. Shape them like a lotus root.

5. Scald the black moss to soften them, shape them like the hair of the lotus root.
6. Knife the tomato into the lotus leaves.
7. Beat the egg white up,
8. Put in chicken mousse and mix them up spread the mixture in the bottom of a dish,
9. Put the lotus flower figure in the dish, and then steam them to be done.
10. Knife the fish tripe into pieces.
11. Scald them in boiling water.
12. Fry the chives and ginger in a frying pot.
13. Put in delicious soup and the seasonings.
14. Braise them together with the shrimp meat, dried scallops, green cabbage hearts, seasonings, delicious soup in the pot until boiling.
15. Take away foam, pour them in a tureen, place the lotus root and flower in it.

Caviar.

Caviar can be defined as an expensive and refined delicacy from sturgeon unfertilized eggs particularly from the beluga species. It was basically obtained by fishermen from the Caspian Sea. Historically, caviar was associated with royalty in Russia and Iran (Persia). It was usually presented as the favorite delicacy to kings and aristocrats such as the Russian Tsar Alexander I.The beluga sturgeon species was threatened by overfishing in the Caspian Sea and the United States of America became the world leader in producing caviar particularly in and around the lakes in the northeast and west. Caviar is readily available in the United States of America; however, it is expensive, making it a delicacy. Caviar is made by sieving and salting large fish roe. Caviar dish has a grainy texture and it is usually served as an appetizer, garnish or spread. Caviar is extremely perishable and must be refrigerated at once after getting the eggs from the fish. I have eaten homemade caviar from tiger and bream. I found them tastier than the fish meat.

Caviar can also be obtained from other seafood creatures such as crabs, urchins, and salmon, shrimp and many more. China and neighboring regions get their caviar from crab and urchin roes and is considered a delicacy. Crab roe are often used as topping in dishes such as "crab roe tofu". Shrimp roes are also consumed as toppings for noodle soup. The following table shows the nutritional value of caviar.

CAVIAR NUTRITIONAL VALUE TABLE.
Protein (25 grams per 100 grams
Potassium (164 mg per 100g)
Vitamin B2
Fat (17 grams per 100 grams)
Phosphorous (330 per 100 g)
Vitamin B44
Cholesterol (440 mg per 100 g)
Calcium (51 mg per 100g)
Vitamin B12
Vitamin A
Vitamin D
Vitamin C
Vitamin PP
Sugar (4 grams per100 grams)
Sodium (1700mg 100g

FRIED FISH EGGS.

Ingredients.
   ¼ kg fish eggs
   1 teaspoon garlic
   2 tablespoons turmeric powder
   3 tablespoons dhania jeera powder or fish masala
   Salt to taste
   1 lemon
   Oil for deep frying
   2 teaspoons red chili paste

Directions.
1. Clean the eggs and remove the hanging skin if any. (Be careful not to tear them, as they are very soft)
2. Cut into 1 1/2 inches pieces.
3. Mix all the spices in a bowl; add little water to make paste.
4. Marinate eggs in this paste slowly and keep for an hour.
5. Deep fry in hot oil till crispy.
6. Serve hot with sauce of your choice or with fries.

Source: Imram (Cook.)

Fish Egg Cakes.

Ingredients.
  2 -3 cups fish cups
  1 medium onion, chopped
  1 egg
  2 tablespoons flour
  ½ teaspoon salt
  Pepper

Directions.
1. Remove eggs from membrane or sack. Don't wash.
2. Add eggs, flour, and pepper and onion.
3. Mix well and drop like small pancakes in medium hot oil or shortening.
4. Turn several times or until brown or well done.

Shark Fins.

China, Japan, and Mexico consider shark fin as a delicacy. Shark fins are obtained from a variety of shark species, for example the dogfish shark. Shark fins are obtained through a process called finning. Sharks are an endangered species in many countries, making it a delicacy because it is a scarce commodity. Animal rights activists criticize shark fin consumption while other people view shark fin eating as an old cultural tradition which dates back to the Ming Dynasty in China in the 18ᵗʰ and 19ᵗʰ centuries. Like caviar, shark fin eating is associated with emperors and aristocrats. The delicacy was coveted by emperors because it was rare, delicious, and required elaborate preparation. Shark fin soups may be served at important cultural functions such as weddings, bouquets, business deals, or at ritual ceremonies. Shark fin symbolizes wealth, power, prestige and honor among the Chinese. The Chinese shark fin gourmet is a show of respect, honor, and appreciation to guests. Some people view shark fin as virtually tasteless but get their taste from the soup ingredients and flavors, and may end up describing the taste as chewy, sinewy or stringy while some say that shark fin taste is somewhere between chewy and crunchy.

The Chinese believe that shark fin possesses some medicinal properties. Chinese culture strongly believe that shark fins have medicinal properties to boost sexual potency, enhance skin quality, and increase one's energy, prevent heart disease, and lower cholesterol. They also believe that shark fins help in areas of rejuvenation of appetite enhancement, and blood nourishment. Shark fin is beneficial to vital energy, kidneys, lungs, bones and many other parts of the body. It has been divulged that vitamin content of typical shark fin soup is much less than that of typical vegetable soup, containing almost no vitamin A. However, it contains slightly more iron, zinc, riboflavin, and phosphorus than normal vegetable soup. Some nutritionists claim that shark fins prevent cancer; however, there is no scientific evidence, and one study found shark cartilage to be of no value in cancer treatment. It is also believed that some restaurants in China are serving artificial shark fin to satisfy their customers' huge shark fin appetite.

Shark Fin Recipes.

SHARK FIN SOUP.

Ingredients.
- 1 ½ gallons of chicken broth
- 1 tablespoon salt to taste
- 1 tablespoon sugar
- ¼ teaspoon white pepper
- 2 fresh ginger, chuck
- 6 ounces shark fin, dried, soak for 1 hour and clean
- 1 cup Dungeness crab
- 1 cup prawns, clean, deveined and minced
- 1 tablespoon soy sauce
- Cornstarch roux
- 1 egg, beaten
- 3 stalks green onions, sliced finely.

Directions.
1. In a large stockpot add broth, salt, sugar, white pepper and ginger and bring to a boil.
2. Reduce the heat to a simmer for 15 minutes.
3. Remove the chuck of gingers. Taste the broth and re-season as needed.
4. Add the shark fin and return back to a simmer.
5. When the shark fin pieces are tender add in the crab meat and prawns.
6. Bring to a boil and add soy sauce.
7. Stir some cornstarch roux to thick the soup.
8. Turn off the heat and stir in the beaten egg and green onion.

By Chef #DBLEE

Chinese Shark's Fin Soup.

Ingredients:

2 tablespoons sesame oil.

4 ounces ready prepared shark's fin, soaked for I hour in cold water and drained.

I spring onion/scallion finely chopped.

8 ounces small shrimps. Peeled.

I inch fresh root ginger, peeled and finely chopped.

1 ½ tablespoons soy sauce.

4 Chinese dried mushrooms, soaked in cold water for 30 minutes, drained and sliced.

1 ½ cornstarch, blended with I tablespoon chicken stock.

2 tablespoons Rice wine.

A dash of black vinegar or brandy (optional.)

2 ¼ quarts or 9 cups chicken stock.

8 ounces boned chicken breast, shredded

Directions:

1. Heat the oil in a pot. Add the spring onion, ginger, mushroom and rice wine and fry for 5 minutes, stirring occasionally.

2. Pour over half the chicken stock, add the shark's fin and bring to boil.

3. Reduce the heat to low and simmer for 10 minutes.

4. Add the chicken, shrimps and soy sauce. Pour the remaining chicken stock and the cornstarch mixture, and bring to the boil, stirring occasionally.

5. Reduce the heat to low again and simmer for another 10 minutes, stirring occasionally.

6. Serve at once with black vinegar or brandy.

Chicken Feet.

Chicken feet are eaten in most countries around the world for example Mexico, China, and Korea, Jamaica, and South Africa, Zimbabwe and many others. Chicken feet, heads, and intestines were usually reserved for young children in Zimbabwe who used them for house play games, known as "mahumbwe"; however, chicken feet are now eaten as part of the main meal because of shortage of beef and high chicken prices. There is little muscle or flesh in chicken feet.Chicken feet is made of skin, cartilage and tendons. This gives the chicken feet a distinct texture different from the rest of the chicken meat. Its small bones make it difficult to eat for some. Chicken feet are very gelatinous. They can be used as a beer snack, cold dish, soup or main dish. It has been observed that the Chinese consumers chew the soft bones and skins of chicken feet and spit out the harder bones. The habit is akin to the consumption of chewing gum, which may satisfy the desire for munching although it does not provide much nutritional value. Below are some suggested ways to clean, prepare and cook chicken feet:

First, you have to cut off the claws and trim of the hard unwanted spot normally seen beneath the feet. Then, rub the chicken feet with salt to clean it thoroughly. Rinse it. Finally, scald the chicken feet in hot boiling water for about 5 minutes. Then the chicken feet is ready to be cooked in any way you want.

Although most cultures consider chicken feet as waste, however, some scientific studies have come up with some amazing chicken feet health benefits, such as ACE inhibitor which helps reduce high blood pressure. Chicken feet contain gelatin and calcium which help lubricate joints and keep our joints in check. Chicken feet also contain collagen which provides the strength of our tissues and organs require while elastin provides the ability to stretch and recoil. Collagen also helps repair some skin damage and helps us look young than our real age.

Chicken Feet.

Chicken Feet (Tswarapasi/Nzondora).Chicken feet consist of skin and tendons, with no muscle.

Chicken Feet Recipes.

CHICKEN FEET SOUP.
1. Bring 2 liters of water to a boil.
2. Put the chicken feet into a large stock pot and cover with boiling water.
3. Boil for 5 minutes. Use a large metal spoon to skim and discard the scum that rises to the surface.
4. Drain the chicken feet completely.

5. Rinse with cold water so that the feet are cool enough to handle.
6. Using a sharp knife chop off the tips of the claws and discard. They should cut easily if you cut them through the joint. If any rough patches of claw pad remain, cut them away with a pairing knife.
7. Place chicken feet in a clean large stockpot.
8. Fill with cold water to cover the feet by 2.5 cm.
9. Add carrots, onions, celery, thyme, bay leaf, and peppercorns.
10. Bring to a simmer, immediately reduce the temperature to low. Partially cover, leave about a half inch crack or so, and keep the stock cooking at a bare simmer, for 4 hours.
11. Occasionally skim any foam that may come to the surface.
12. Uncover, increase the heat slightly to maintain a low simmer with the pot now uncovered.
13. Continue to cook for an hour or two.
14. At this point you are reducing the stock so that it is easier to store.
15. Strain the stock through several layers of cheesecloth or a fine mesh strainer (ideally both) into a pot.
16. Pour into quart-sized jars.
17. Let cool for an hour or so before storing in the refrigerator.
18. When the stock has cooled, it should firm up nicely into a gel.

Gizzards (Chikanganwahama/Chihururu).

Poultry gizzards are a popular food and delicacy throughout the world for example in Haiti, Southeast Asia and some African countries like Zimbabwe, South Africa, and Zambia. The gizzard is an organ found in the digestive tract of some birds for example the ostrich and chicken. The gizzard can be described as poultry specialized stomach constructed of thick, muscular walls used for grinding up food; often small stones are instrumental in this process. Bird gizzards are lined with a tough layer made of the carbohydrate-protein complex koilin to protect the muscles in the gizzard and to aid in digestion. In Mainland China, duck gizzard is a common snack, eaten alongside other duck parts such as feet, neck, heart, tongue, or head.

In Zimbabwe, gizzards are also known as "chikanganwa hama or chihururu" are culturally served to fathers as heads of households. Children are strictly prohibited from eating gizzards. They are however, served chicken feet, heads, and intestines, liver hearts, and other waste. It is believed that children may forget their relatives (kanganwa Hama) if they eat gizzards or they may become mean. Gizzards are also a popular pub snack.

Some scientific studies have proved that poultry gizzards have some health benefits such as control weight because they are low in calories, control high blood pressure because gizzards are low in sodium. It has also been proved that eating gizzards also prevents some nutritional deficiencies, for example eating gizzards promote heart health because gizzards are an excellent source of selenium which supports antioxidant activity of Vitamins C and E. It has also been proved that eating gizzards promotes health immune system because they contain zinc and essential minerals.

ANDREW NYAKUPFUKA

Recipes.

CHICKEN GIZZARDS.

Ingredients.
  1 pound chicken gizzards
  ¼ cup butter
  Salt and pepper to taste
  Water

Directions.
1. Place gizzards in a saucepan with enough water to cover by 1 inch.
2. Bring to a boil over medium heat, cover, and cook for 1 1/2 hours.
3. Drain and chop into bite size pieces.
4. Melt butter in a large skillet over medium-high heat.
5. Fry gizzards in butter for about 15 minutes.
6. Season with salt and pepper to taste.

Fried Gizzards.

Ingredients.
- 1 ½ pounds chicken gizzards
- ½ cup all –purpose flour
- 1 ½ teaspoon seasoned salt
- 1 ½ teaspoon ground black pepper
- 1 ½ garlic powder
- 2 cups vegetable oil for frying

Directions.
1. Trim excess fat and gristle from chicken gizzards. Rinse under cold running water.
2. Place gizzards in a pot of cold water. Bring water and gizzards to a rolling boil; continue to boil for about 15 minutes.
3. Strain gizzards using a colander. Allow to cool.
4. Meanwhile, combine the flour, seasoned salt, pepper, and garlic powder in a plastic bag. Shake well to combine.
5. Preheat vegetable oil in a skillet with a lid over medium-high heat to 375 degrees F (190 degrees C).
6. Thoroughly coat gizzards with flour mixture and shake off excess.
7. Gently lay the coated gizzards in the hot oil. Cook until brown.
8. Reduce heat to medium; cover skillet with lid and cook another 10 minutes.
9. Remove to paper towels to drain.

Duck Tongue.

Chichi Wang (My Chalkboard, Blog) said that the duck tongue is surrounded by a faint hint of meat and papery thin layers of cartilage; the duck tongue is predominately made of juicy pockets of fat. It is barely two inches in length, the tongue may seem small and insubstantial, but its flavor is intensely ducklike. Unlike that of mammals, the duck tongue possesses a bone that runs throughout the middle of the organ. Instead of being covered on top in taste buds, tiny papillae protrude on either side of the tongue. While the tongue of cows and pigs are muscle meat, varying only somewhat in texture from the flesh on bones, the tongues of ducks bear no resemblance to duck meat.

Recipes.

DEEP-FRIED DUCK TONGUE.

Ingredients.
    1 pound duck tongue, rinsed and dried
    2 teaspoons soy sauce
    1 teaspoon rice wine
    ½ teaspoon white pepper
    Chile sauce or cayenne pepper to taste
    ½ egg white beaten
    1 table spoon cornstarch
    2 cups oil, for frying
    Salt

Directions.
1. To prepare the marinade: Combine the soy sauce, rice wine, white pepper, and chili sauce in a bowl. Add the duck

tongues and mix evenly. Leave them in the marinade for half an hour, turning occasionally.

2. Remove the duck tongues from the mixture, but do not wipe dry.

3. Add the egg white and the cornstarch to the duck tongues and mix evenly.

4. Meanwhile, bring the oil to 350°F at the base of a wok. Gently slip the duck tongues into the oil, taking care not to splash the surface.

5. Stir the tongues around slowly in the oil to prevent sticking.

6. Deep-fry 1 to 2 minutes, until the tongues are golden-brown and crisp.

7. Remove the tongues from the wok and let them blot briefly on a paper towel. (Depending on how much oil you want to use, cook the tongues in batches.)

8. Serve while crisp and piping hot

Source: Chichi Wang.

Duck Tongue Soup Recipe

Ingredients.
- 24 ducks
- 2 slices ginger
- 1 stalk scallion, cut into 1 inch sections
- 1 teaspoon salt
- 1 tablespoon sherry
- 6 cups chicken stock
- 1/8 teaspoon pepper

Directions.
1. Place the tongues, ginger, scallion and half of the salt in a bowl.
2. Place on a rack in a saucepan filled up to 2 inches of water and steam for 1 hour.
3. Bring the chicken stock to a boil
4. Add the rest of the ingredients with the ducks tongues.
5. When it comes to a boil, correct the seasoning.
6. Serve in a deep bowl.

Blood. (Musiya).

Some people the world over eat or drink blood from slaughtered domesticated animals such as cattle, goats, and sheep as a food or as a delicacy, for example the Masai people in Tanzania do not necessarily kill their cattle to get the blood, they get the blood directly from the neck of the live animal and the wound is allowed to heal. They mix the blood with milk and drink the mixture.

Zimbabweans, on the other hand consume beef, hog, and goat blood known as "musiya" mixed with some offal such as tripe, lungs, and intestines, hearts, fat, and pancreas and cooked. Cooked ox blood looks like black pudding. This dish is only eaten by males of all ages. It is prepared and cooked at the place where the animal was slaughtered. Women are prohibited to cook this dish on the cultural beliefs that they would have problems with their monthly periods. I have actually eaten this dish. It is tasty but over eating the cooked blood may cause severe diarrhea. In other cultures, the blood could be in the form of blood sausage as a thickener for sauces, a cured salted form in times of food shortages or in a blood soup. It is taboo to eat or drink animal blood in some cultures or religions, for an example Jews and Moslems do not eat or drink animal blood in whatever form because of religious dietary laws.

Duck Blood.

Nanjing people in China are renowned for their appetite for ducks meat, including their viscera; even the duck blood can be utilized. There is this funny folklore which justifies the eating of duck blood. It is said that once there was a poor man in Nanjing. He killed a duck and used a bowl to hold the duck's blood. But he dropped the vermicelli into the bowl carelessly. So he had to cook them together and surprisingly found that the soup was delicious. The landlord heard that and employed the poor man to be his cook and cook that kind of dish for his family. Afterwards, the dish was named as duck blood and vermicelli soup, and has been popular ever since. Zimbabweans do eat any poultry blood. However, some traditional healers use poultry blood to cure certain ailments or conditions such as some bad luck or cleansing patients afflicted by avenging spirits known as "ngozi."

Recipe.

DUCK BLOOD AND VERMICELLI SOUP.

Vermicelli is made of sweet potato. It is smooth, soft, waxy and tasty.

Ingredients
  Duck blood
  Vermicelli
  Dried tofu
  Dried shrimp
  Duck gizzards
  Duck intestines
  Shallots
  Ginger
  Sesame oil
  Caraway
  Salt
  Duck livers

Instructions.
1. Cut the curdled duck blood into small cubes.
2. Boil duck gizzards, intestines, and livers until cooked.
3. Fish out the duck gizzards, intestines, and livers and cut them into small pieces.
4. Permeate sweet potatoes (vermicelli) into warm water in order to make them soft for later cooking.
5. Put duck liver, duck blood and vermicelli, ginger sauce, vinegar, dried shrimp and dried tofu in a big bowl and boil for a few minutes.

6. Add sesame oil and salt to taste.
7. Evenly distribute pieces of shallot and caraway for color and fragrance.

Pig Blood.

Recipe.

PORK DINUGUAN.
1 kg of pork belly, cut into small cubes
350g of pork liver
4c. of pigs blood
3 chili peppers (sling haba)
1 head of garlic, crushed and minced
1 thumb –sized piece of ginger, minced
3 onions, halved and sliced thinly
1 pound of sinigang mix good for 1 liter of broth
1 bay leaf
Salt
Pepper (optional)
1 tablespoon cooking oil

Instructions.
1. Refrigerate the pig's blood until needed.
2. Heat a heavy casserole.
3. Pour in the cooking oil. When the oil starts to smoke, add the garlic and ginger.
4. Sauté until fragrant.

5. Add the pork pieces and cook over high heat until the edges of the pork start to brown.
6. Add the onions, chili peppers, bay leaf and sinigang mix and continue cooking until the onions are transparent.
7. Season with salt and pepper, if using.
8. Pour in just enough water to cover.
9. Bring to a boil, lower the heat, cover and simmer for 30-45 minutes or until the pork is very tender.
10. Add more water, a little at a time, if the liquid dries up before the pork is cooked.
11. Add minced t liver.
12. Season with a little salt.
13. When the pork is tender and most of the liquid has evaporated, take the pig's blood out of the refrigerator.
14. Transfer to a clean bowl. With your hands, mash solid masses to a pulp. Pour the mashed blood and the liquid into the casserole. Bring to a boil.
15. Cook over medium heat, stirring, for about 5 minutes. Add the minced liver and cook for another minute or two.
16. Add more salt if necessary.
17. Serve the Dinuguan hot with sweet rice cakes or steamed rice.

Deer Penis.

A deer penis is said to have important therapeutic properties in traditional Chinese medicine. Like turtle's blood and penis, deer penis is one of the "delicacies" served in large jars in Chinese restaurants. The deer penis is typically very large and, proponents claim, for it to retain its properties it must be extracted from the deer whilst still alive. It is sliced into small pieces by women and then roasted and dried in the sun. Eating deer penis is said to enhance sexual potency in men. The penis of a deer, turtle or bull is also consumed in Singapore. Women in Singapore are reported as eating deer penis during pregnancy as it is said to have a fattening effect and to make the mother and child stronger. It is offensive to eat any animal penis in some cultures; however, I feel it is by choice.

Trotters.

Trotters can be defined as pig's feet; however, some cultures include goats' or sheep's feet to this definition. I have observed that most Americans do not eat trotters, however quite a good number of cultures around the world enjoy trotters which they view as a delicacy. They actually employ a variety of recipes to make them more palatable or tasty, for example, prior to sale, the trotters are cleaned, and the hairs are removed by the use of a hot tank and beaters or by burning off the hairs. They are cooked for a long period, may be at least two to three hours on an open fire. They may add tomatoes and onions. There is no need to add cooking oil as trotters have enough fat. Trotters are gelatinous. Trotters can be served as a normal cut of meat or a snack or a flavor. Pickled pig's feet is a type of pork associated with of the Southern United States, African American soul food cuisine.

Trotters have a high fat content, with almost an equal portion of saturated fat to protein. Some people prefer to preserve trotters by salting and smoking. Trotters can also be preserved the same way as home canning and processes for pickled vegetables; typically a saturation of hot vinegar brine is used.

Pig's feet or trotters are eaten in Zimbabwe as a delicacy or a snack by ale imbibers. However, due to the prohibitive cost of pork and beef some families go along with trotters as a source of protein. Some people in Zimbabwe and the world over do not eat pork on religious grounds. The "mapositori" literary (apostles) in Zimbabwe do not eat pork on the basis of the kosher dietary laws. I have sampled trotters, I find them appealing. However, my family does not like them. There are different ways of cooking trotters. Here are some suggested trotters recipes.

Recipe.

PICKLED PIG'S FEET II

Ingredients
    6 pig's feet
    2 fresh red chilies
    2 tablespoons salt
    2 cups white vinegar

Directions
1. In a large stainless steel pot, place pig's feet and enough water to cover.
2. Boil feet 2 hours or until tender.
3. Drain. Rinse feet in hot water to remove excess fat.
4. Remove as many bones as you can.
5. Put 1 chili pepper and 3 pig's feet in each one quart jar.

6. In a separate bowl, mix salt and vinegar together.
7. Pour vinegar mixture over pig's feet to cover.
8. Seal jars and refrigerate for at least 3 days to 1 week before eating.

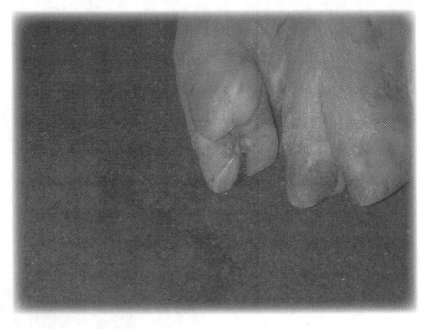

Pig's Feet/Trotters. Trotters have a high fat content.

Nozki.

Nozki is a Polish delicacy made of jellied pig's feet or trotters. Nozki is not as repulsive as it sounds. The meat is simmered with herbs and spices until falling off the bone, and set in gelatin.

Smalahove.

Smalahove is a Western Norwegian traditional dish made from a sheep's head, originally eaten before Christmas. Smalahove was typically eaten by the poor, but today it is considered a delicacy.

The skin and fleece of the head is torched, the brain removed, and the head is salted sometimes smoked, and dried. The head is boiled or steamed for about three hours and served with mashed rutabaga and potatoes. In some preparations, the brain is cooked inside the skull and then eaten with a spoon or fried

Pig Intestines.

Pig intestines are known as "makchang" (Korean) is usually grilled over a barbecue, but preparation has to be done beforehand to rid the meat of odd odors and excessive fat. Most Zimbabweans do not eat pork or pork intestines and the gut especially in rural areas where hogs are left to roam around the village and eat whatever, they come across. Hogs can eat anything they can find including dirt or human feces. People feel they may be affected by tape worms or contract some diseases. The Koreans may either be pre-boil pork intestines in water seasoned with "doenjan", onions, medicinal herbs, or pre-marinated in a sauce made of various fruit such as apple, Korean pear, pineapple, kiwi, and many others before grilling. The dipping sauce is made from a mixture of "doenjang", ground beans, ground red pepper, and chopped scallions. Fresh green and red peppers, cucumbers, minari and garlic are sometimes added according to personal taste.

How to Prepare Deep Fried Crispy Pig Intestines.

Ingredients.

Pig intestines cut into manageable lengths.

Vegetable oil for deep frying.

Salt to taste.

Method.

1. Clean the pig intestines using running water or a large bowl of water.

2. Heat the wok and put in the pig intestines and turn the heat low.

3. Cover the wok as pig intestines tend to explode when deep fried.

4. Fry until the intestines turn golden brown

5. Remove the pig intestines from the wok and drain excess oil.

6. Sprinkle some salt on the crispy pig intestines and mix well.

7. Serve with "sadza", or as a snack.

Blubber (Mafuta).

Blubber and seal flippers are considered delicacies in Japan. Blubber can be defined as a thick layer of fat below a whale's or seal's skin that helps to keep them warm when they swim through cold ocean waters. This insulating layer is the only thing keeping these marine animals from freezing to death. Blubber is also used to store the much needed energy for future use. Blubber is consumed in such countries and islands as Norway, Iceland, and the Foroe Islands.

Seal liver and blubber are excellent sources of vitamin "A" and vitamin "C".The Inuit consider seal meat and organs as "special food" that keeps them healthy and warm. Seal meat is also used as a medicine to heal the body and soul from sickness. The Inuit also believe that blubber has some medicinal properties which help cure cardiac ailments. Ringed seal liver is a major source of selenium in the Inuit diet; along with "beluga maktaag" (skin and blubber).It is believed that blubber tastes like arrowroot biscuit.

Blubber can be used to make "whale oil" which can be used as soap and a component in makeup that contributes a glossy shine. Blubber is also turned into fuel for lamps, wax for candles and grease for machinery. Sperm whale oil is favored for lamps because it burns slowly and does not emit bad odors. However, it is believed that blubber contains naturally carcinogens that damage humans' nervous, immune and reproductive systems.

Out of the Blubber.

You clean the blubber (fat) from the skin and cut the blubber in strips about 2 by 6 inches and put them in clean barrel and put loose cover on barrel and put the barrel with blubber in dry place where there is no heat. Pretty soon that blubber will dissolve and become oil and then it will be ready to use with meat or diced fish or green leaves.

Source: Mary Milbury.
Anchorage, Alaska.

Kokoretsi.

Kokoretsi or kokoreç is a dish of the Balkans, notably in Greece consisting mainly of lamb or goat intestines, often wrapping seasoned offal, including sweetbreads, hearts, lungs or kidneys. The intestines of suckling lambs are preferred. The intestines are turned inside out and carefully washed and rubbed thoroughly with coarse salt and then soaked in vinegar or lemon juice and water. Kokoretsi is usually roasted on a horizontal skewer over a charcoal, gas, or electrical burner.

ANDREW NYAKUPFUKA

Rodents

Rabbit.

Judith Wilson in her article, "What are Rodents?" defines rodents as one of the most prolific and adaptable groups of mammals, accounting for over a third of all mammal species. They include burrowing, grazing, arboreal and aquatic species. Several rodents have successfully adapted to living alongside humans, although they are not always welcome. The rodents' family includes squirrels, mice, and guinea pigs, coypus and porcupines. The less familiar rodents include "springhaas" and scaly-tailed squirrels. Despite appearances, rodents are more closely related to other placental mammals such as humans and cows, than to marsupials such as possums.

Rabbits are small mammals found in several parts of the world including Zimbabwe.Rabbit meat is not very popular in Zimbabwe because most people do not engage in backyard butcheries, besides most people do not have the requisite knowledge to rear rabbits as an enterprising commercial venture. Rural folks use dogs to hunt for wild hares but it is very difficult to come across one because their habit has been turned into farmland and other land uses. I have eaten a lot of rabbit meat because I used to keep them at my property. My father was a traditional hunter who used to bring a lot of bush meat including hare.

It has been recorded that more than half of the rabbit population resides in North America. Rabbits are herbivores that feed by grazing on grass, forbs, and leafy weeds. Rabbits live in groups in underground burrows, or rabbit holes. A cluster of burrows is called a warren. The male is called a buck and the female is a doe while the young one is a kitten or kit. Rabbits are raised for pets, show, and laboratory testing, pelts, and Angora wool, and meat. Rabbit meat is considered a delicacy by many cultures in Africa especially in Morocco. Rabbit meat is low in fat, high in protein.

A Rabbit. (Tsuro) Rabbit meat is considered a delicacy by many cultures in Africa especially in Morocco.

Rabbit Recipe.

Rabbit Stew.

Ingredients

I rabbit sectioned
2 medium carrots diced
I medium onion diced
I large glass good red wine
I large can of whole tomatoes in juice
¼ teaspoon rabbit seasoning
I gravy stock cube
2 bay leaves
I medium can peas
I ½ teaspoon dried mint
I medium can peas
Corn flour to thicken
Salt to taste

Method.

1. Lightly fry the rabbit until it is brown all over.
2. Fry the carrots and onion together in a large pan.
3. Toss in the rabbit and wine.
4. add water until the rabbit is covered.
5. Add curry, rabbit seasoning, mint, stock cube and bay leaves.
6. Stir everything together and bring to boil.
7. Simmer for about I to 11/2 hours.
8. Blend some corn flour with cold water and stir until you have nice thick gravy.
9. Add the peas and stir.

By Claire Camilleri

Guinea Pig.

Guinea pigs are rare in Zimbabwe; some people have never seen them. However, they have seen the guinea pig's relative known in the local language as "mbira" which lives in the wild particularly in caves and among outcrops. The wild guinea pig is threatened by agricultural land use and home construction. Those Zimbabweans who have access to guinea pig are not very kin to eat it may be because of its appearance. They are very difficult to catch or trap. I have eaten the wild guinea pig, and found the meat tasty especially if it dried and cooked with peanut butter. . Guinea pig also known as "cuy" was originally domesticated for their meat in the Andes Mountains. Guinea pigs were traditionally reserved for ceremonial meals. However, guinea pigs meat has become a delicacy in some Latin American countries such as Peru, Bolivia, Ecuador and Colombia.

Guinea-Pig Recipe.

OVEN ROASTED GUINEA PIG

Ingredients
  Guinea pig meat
  Water
  Tomato Avocado
  Potato
  Plantains

Instructions.
1. Cut the meat of the bone
2. Rub the meat with salt to taste
3. Wrap the pieces of meat in banana leaves and fold leaves

4. Tie the folded leaves with kitchen string
5. Place in a roasting pan
6. Pour 4 cups of water over the folded leaves
7. Place in oven for 3 hours on a low heat
8. Add potatoes and a little more water and cook for another hour
9. Unwrap the folded leaves and scoop the guinea pig meat
10. Serve with plantains, sweet potatoes, and gravy, raw tomato or avocados

A dish of roasted Guinea Pig in Ecuador
Photographer: Sascha Grabow.

Squirrel.

Squirrels are indigenous to the Americas, Europe, and Asia, Australia and Africa. They breed once or twice a year and give birth to a varying number of young after a gestation period of three to six weeks. The young are born naked, toothless, and blind. In most species of squirrel, only the female looks after the young, which are weaned at around six to ten weeks of age. The young ones become sexually mature at the end of their first year. Squirrels are generally social animals; however, the tree-dwelling species are more solitary. Squirrels are typically diurnal while flying squirrels tend to be nocturnal.

Squirrels' diets consist primarily of a wide variety of plants, including nuts, seeds, conifer cones, fruits, fungi and green vegetation. However, it has been observed that some squirrels also consume meat, especially when faced with hunger. Squirrels have been known to eat insects, eggs, small birds, young snakes and smaller rodents.

The gray squirrel meat and brain is regarded as a delicacy in Britain and in the southern states of the United States of America. The squirrel brain can serve as nourishment just as the pig, horse, and cattle, monkeys, chicken, and goats are. Britain's Telegraph (06/03/ 2008) reported that gray squirrel meat is in such high demand that game butchers are struggling to keep up with demand. Squirrel has been praised for its low fat content and for being "green," since it comes from local, "free range," sources. Chefs say that squirrel meat tastes like wild rabbit or game, is dark and usually slow-cooked before being made in casseroles, hot-pots or pies.

Squirrel Recipes.

CAJUN SQUIRREL.

Ingredients.
   Squirrels cut into serving pieces.
   I large green bell pepper.
   2 cloves garlic.
   Cajun spice.
   2 tablespoon Tabasco soup.
   Water.
   4 tablespoons ketchup
   I tablespoon Gumbo File seasoning
   Cooked rice.
   Olive oil.
   Cooked rice

Directions.
1. Heat some olive oil in a deep pot or Dutch oven.
2. Season the squirrel on all sides with Cajun seasoning.
3. Add the hot and turn to brown on all sides.
4. Continue to cook until done.
5. Place the onion, bell pepper and garlic in a blender.
6. 6. Cover with water and chop.
7. 7. Add to the pot when squirrel is done.
8. 8. Sprinkle the added vegetables with Cajun seasoning.
9. 9. Add the Tabasco sauce, ketchup and Gumbo File.
10. 10. Serve over the cooked rice.

Source: Connie Dupont.

Gray Squirrel (Tsindi/Shindi): Squirrel
meat tastes like wild rabbit or game.

Andrew Nyakupfuka

Squirrel Recipes.

Campfire Roasted Squirrel.

Ingredients.
- 4 -6 fresh squirrels
- ¼ teaspoon salt
- ¼ teaspoon pepper
- ¼ cup olive oil
- ¼ teaspoon seasoning salt (optional)
- ¼ teaspoon Creole seasoning (optional)

Instructions.
1. If fresh squirrel is used skin and leave whole splitting the breast bone length wise to open up the rib cage.
2. Brush the oil over the squirrel then sprinkle the seasonings liberally.
3. Pull the hot coals to one side from the main part of the fire.
4. Either stake the squirrel on a cleaned tree limb over the coals or use a metal grate over the coals.
5. Rotate periodically and do not overcook as the meat is real lean and will dry out fast.

FRIED SQUIRREL.

Ingredients.
   I squirrel
   Butter, melted as needed for the size
   Corn flakes, crushed as needed
   Cooking oil or shortening or bacon grease as needed

Instructions.
1. Remove legs from body of dressed rabbit or squirrel.
2. Split the body down the back through the breast.
3. Cut each half in two crosswise.
4. Dip meat pieces in melted butter.
5. Roll pieces into crushed corn flakes coating all around.
6. Brown meat in hot oil on each side.
7. Reduce heat to low and simmer for about I hour.
8. If so cover the body with water in a pot and add 3 Tablespoons of salt.
9. Then drain, rinse, and pat the body dry before cooking.

Note: Some people like to soak the meat in salted water a few hours before cooking.

Source: Chuck Killbuck.

Mice.

Most people in my village eat mice. Those who do not eat mice, it is by choice or by religious dietary law such as Christians. We nickname dried and roasted mice "sausages" because they look like sauasages.Most people in Mozambique, Zambia, and Malawi eat mice. It is speculated that the most famous snack in Malawi is roasted field mice. Most people in these countries are largely divided as to the culinary merit of mice. Most love mice and consider them a seasonal delicacy however, people of the Ndebele tribe in Zimbabwe do not eat mice on cultural grounds. Mice are usually caught or trapped in winter and spring. People, particularly children and women dig them out from their burrows, trap them or catch them while harvesting corn. Mice usually stay in burrows and corn sheafs.However, my local people are wary to select mice from rats. They do not eat rats. Mice are found in the wild especially corn fields as they mostly feed on grain, nuts and seeds. Rats are found in people's homes. Rats are shunned and believed to carry diseases such as bubonic plague. However, some people eat both rats and mice. Mice are caught and roasted over a fire, but not roasted long enough to burn off the copious amounts of visible fur then garnish them with salt and cayenne pepper and gnaw on them like jerky, consuming them completely, bones and all. Alternatively mice can be consumed with sadza.Mice are also consumed as pub lunch.

Mice are also consumed as a delicacy in other parts of the world particularly in China. Here is a rather disgusting and cruel way of eating the young ones in China. There is a practice called "Chirping three times", which originally arose in Guangzhou and then spread to Beijing. In this way of eating, people dine the newly-born mice. As they pick up the mouse with chopsticks, it gives out the "first cry". Then dipping it in the seasoning juice, it makes a "second cry". At last, it cries while being bitten.

Mouse.

Prebles Jumping Mouse (Mbewa). Zimbabweans
consume mice as a snack or relish with "sadza".

Catching Mice

There are several traditional ways of catching mice. Some use
the traditional laborious way of digging them out or using some flat
stone traps (mariva).However some now using modern technology
like rat traps. Place the glue traps in the places where mice have
been noticed especially in corn fields. Place them near corn stakes.
It's best to place several traps together, or to buy the rat-size traps.
Bait the traps. Some pest-control companies manufacture a bait
product designed for this purpose, but mouse-alluring food such
as a dab of peanut butter is effective.

How to cook Mice/Rats.

Prepared mice/rats can be skewered on a greenish stick and held over a fire for a few minutes. The main thing to be concerned with at this point is not burning them, so take special care, and rotate them a few times, constantly checking they are cooking nicely. Depending on the size, they can take from three to ten minutes. Mice/rats can be seasoned to taste. If you need to store some of the meat, you can also smoke them. This is a good way to save some of the meat for later use as it should last between one and four weeks depending on how long you smoked it for. Use hard, green wood, not resinous ones as this will ruin the meat. Make sure none of the carcasses are touching.

Carnivore Pets.

Dog Meat.

IT IS TABOO AND anathema to eat dog meat in most parts of Africa, for example, Zimbabwe and its neighboring countries. Zimbabweans keep hunting dogs or as pets. People who reside in high density suburbs are prohibited from keeping dogs by the local authorities as most of them cannot afford to maintain them due to limited funds and space. However, the practice of eating dog meat is slowly creeping in because of the avalanche of Chinese entrepreneurs in Zimbabwe. It is strongly believed that some business people have consumed dog meat knowingly or unknowingly because of their business trips to China. Some people are rounding up some stray dogs and selling them to the Chinese.

However, I was made to believe that some tribes in Malawi eat dog meat. I failed to verify this assertion. I was told that they eat dog meat under the false name as "mbudzi maunje" literally meaning a wild goat .It has also been recorded that some tribes in west Africa eat dog meat for example the Vame people, eat dog meat for specific rituals, the Tallensi, in Ghana consider dog meat as a delicacy. It is speculated that the Mamprusi in Ghana only eat dog meat as a "courtship stew" provided by a king to his royal lineage. Dogs are also eaten by various groups in some states of Nigeria, for example the Taraba and Gombe tribes. It has been speculated that dog meat is listed as "404" in some Nigerian restaurants' menu to avoid the stigma of eating dog meat. The dog's head is also considered a delicacy in some parts of Nigeria.

It is documented that human consumption of dog meat was prevalent in many parts of the world, including ancient China, ancient Mexico, and ancient Rome. China is the greatest purveyor in eating and distributing dog meat. Dog meat is also popular and consumed in modern countries such as Switzerland, China, Vietnam, and Korea. Dog meat can be consumed in different forms for example dog meat can be consumed as stew, soup, and barbecue, jerky, and snack. Some entrepreneurs use it in making sandwiches and sausages. Some cultures view the consumption of dog meat to be a delicacy and a part of their traditional cuisine, while others consider consumption of dog meat to be inappropriate, offensive, and disgusting on both social and religious grounds.

Dog meat is believed to have medicinal properties. It is popular in winter months, as it is believed to generate heat and promote bodily warmth during cold months. It has been reported that Chinese astronauts consume dog meat while in outer space. The Vietnamese believe that dog meat increases virility in a man. The Koreans also say that eating dog improves women's skin texture, is cure for summer heat, and it is recommended if one is suffering from an illness. Many nutritionists argue that all these purported medicinal benefits have no scientific proof. Dog meat is rarely eaten in New Zealand but has been said to be becoming more popular as it isn't illegal as long as the dog is humanely killed.

Smoked Dog Meat. (Imbwa). A dog meat platter found
in a street market in east Hanoi. Dog meat is believed
to bring good fortune in Vietnam. Dog meat is also
believed to have some medicinal properties in Uzbekistan
while dog meat is a delicacy in East Timor.

Photographer: Viet Grant.

ANDREW NYAKUPFUKA

Dog meat recipes.

Deep-Fried Stuffing On A Stick

Ingredients.
Stuffing.
5 tablespoon butter, divided.
I pound breakfast sausage, bulk.
I cup diced onion.
½ cup diced celery.
I bag unseasoned bread cubes, for stuffing
I sleeve crackers, crushed.
I tablespoon poultry seasoning
2 tablespoons dried parsley flakes.
2 tablespoons ground sage.
Salt and freshly ground pepper.
I quart chicken stock.
4 eggs, beaten

For Frying.
Oil for frying
2 cups all purpose flour
Special equipment: I2 wooden ice cream sticks or skewers

Directions.
1. Preheat oven to 375 degrees F.
2. Grease a 9 by I3-inch baking dish with I tablespoon of the butter.
3. Brown the sausage in a large skillet over medium-high heat until it is cooked through.
4. Transfer to a plate, while spooning off the excess grease, leaving about 2 tablespoons in the skillet.

5. Add 4 tablespoons of the butter and melt.
6. Add the onion, carrot and celery and sauté until softened.
7. Meanwhile, in a large mixing bowl, toss together bread cubes, saltines, poultry seasoning, parsley flakes, sage, salt and pepper.
8. Stir the sautéed vegetables into the mixing bowl.
9. Pour in the chicken stock and eggs and toss together.
10. Turn the stuffing out into the prepared baking dish.
11. Bake in the preheated oven for 35 to 45 minutes until the top is golden brown and the juices in the stuffing are bubbling.
12. Preheat oil in the deep-fryer to 350 degrees F.
13. Cool the stuffing completely. Cut it into 12 squares.
14. Remove each square from the dish and wrap it around a wooden stick, pressing it onto the stick with your hands.
15. Make the stuffing form a log shape around the Popsicle stick, leaving 2-inches of the stick exposed for the handle. This should look somewhat like a lumpy corn dog.
16. Roll the stick in the flour, coating it well and then shaking off the excess.
17. Gently lower the sticks into the hot oil and fry until golden brown and crispy, about 5 minutes.
18. Transfer to a paper towel lined plate to drain.
19. 12 servings.

Source: Recipe courtesy Paula Deen, 2007.

Cuisine of Dog Meat.

BOSINTANG (SOUP).

Ingredients.
  100 g of boiled dog meat.
  500 g of gravy.
  20 g of green onion
  10 g of a leek
  10 g of perilla leaves
  100 g of taro stalk soaked in water
  (2) Sauce
  100 g boiled dog meat
  2 g of mashed garlic
  3 g of perilla leaves
  2 g of red pepper
  2 g of mashed ginger
  A little amount of pepper.

Instruction
1. After boiling the meat with gravy and stalk of taro for some time.
2. Boil again after putting vegetables and other ingredients into it.
3. Before eating, sprinkle pepper on it and put into an earthen bowl.
4. The stalk of taro is to be kept in cold water one or two days to get rid of its smell and taste.

How to Cook Lemongrass Dog.

Ingredients.
  2 pounds dog meat
  4 -3 feet stalks of lemongrass
  3 tablespoons Vietnamese fish source
  2 teaspoons lime juice
  ½ teaspoon lime zest
  Jasmine rice (if desired)
  Rice vermicelli (if desired)
  Baguette (if desired)

Directions.
1. Acquire two pounds of dog meat.Try to ensure that it is from a medium-sized dog. The breed does not matter, unless you have certain preferences.
2. Mince four 3-feet stalks of fresh lemongrass. (Alternatively, use an 8 oz. package of frozen minced lemongrass
3. Mix the minced lemongrass with three tablespoons of Vietnamese fish sauce, two teaspoons of lime juice, and a half teaspoon of lime zest. A recommended brand is Three Crabs Brand, but all in all, fish sauce tends to taste the same.
4. Chop the dog meat into 1-inch pieces. Add the lemongrass marinade and stir. Leave the mixture refrigerated overnight.
5. Either sauté, steam, or grill the meat. A recommended way to cook this dish is to skewer the meat chunks and roast it in a rotisserie oven.

Cat.

Cat meat is eaten in certain cultures around the world for example Swiss, Chinese, Korean, and Japanese, Peruvian, and Brazilian cultures. Some cultures eat cat meat and the offal while others do not eat cat offal. Cat meat may be consumed as barbecue, jerky, and snack or meatballs served with soup. In Guangdong, cat meat is a main ingredient in the traditional dish "dragon, tiger, phoenix" (snake, cat, chicken), which is said to fortify the body. The Japanese have been eating cat meat since the end of Tokugawa period in the 19th century .It is also believed that in Korea, cat meat used to be boiled and made into a tonic as a folk remedy for neuralgia and arthritis. The meat by itself is not customarily eaten. Cat is not a regular menu item in Peru, but it is used in such dishes as fricassee and stews most abundant in two specific sites in the country such as Chincha Alta and Andean, where cat meat is consumed as a replacement for guinea pig. In some parts of Brazil such as Rio de Janeiro cat meat is used as barbeque and for making sausages popularly known in local language as "churrasquinho de gato" literally meaning cat barbeque. Some cultures in Brazil believe that eating cat meat will bring good luck or health.

Cats' by - products for example cat pelts, dog meat and dog skins are also creeping into the European market. It is strongly believed that dogs' and cats' skins are being traded using pseudonyms such as wild cat, katzenfelle, and rabbit, goyang, and mountain cat fur. These false brand names are used to remove the stigma associated with cats. Cats are associated with bad luck and witchcraft particularly the black cat. The practice of marketing in cats' fur and dogs' skins assertion was reported by Hartwell S. (2003 -2005) a BBC reporter. He frequently reported that hundreds of thousands of cat and dog skins were traded in Europe each year. It was further reported that a Belgian furrier appeared on video displaying a fur blanket apparently made from cats farmed in Belgium. He claimed that stray cats and dogs in the area were rounded up, slaughtered and skinned. It is also believed that restrictions on seal culling have led to an increased use of cat fur in the manufacture of cuddly toys and ornaments. Patterned cat fur 'tabby or spotted' is fast replacing that of ocelot and leopard. It is further alleged that some European entrepreneurs are contemplating importing cat fur or starting cat fur companies in Australia which has a large feral cat population. Cat fur is considered a potentially marketable product with the income helping to fund the feral elimination programs in Australia.

Cat Meat Recipes.

Preparation.

Fur is removed from cats after slaughter. Cats are submerged in boiling water for a few seconds after being killed. This loosens the fur, making it easier to remove. Cat may not be the most glamorous, or tastiest of game meats, but with a little thought and preparation, Baked Cat can make the belly of the diner glow with home baked goodness.

Beer Roasted Cat

Instructions.

1 cat cut into roast
1 can of mushroom soup
1 cube of bouillon
1 clove of garlic
1 Fine Irish Stout, like Guinness

Directions

1. Cover and soak cat roast in salt water for 24 hours.
2. Drain water and then cover and soak in beer for 6 hours.
3. Drain and place in crock pot with your cans of soup.
4. Add a clove of garlic, and a cube of beef bouillon.
5. If you start to slow cook your cat in the morning with your George Foreman Cooker (or its ilk), you'll have finely cooked feline in time for supper.
6. If a slow cooker is not available, a cat can be baked at 350 degrees for 2-3 hours in a conventional oven and still come out pretty good.
7. Beer Roasted Cat is fantastic served with mashed potatoes, collard greens, and fresh, homemade egg rolls. When planning a full meal just remember- cat is a course best served hot!

Cat Stew.

Please remember to defur, declaw, and debone the cat before adding to pot. (This may take a while.)

Ingredients
   Cat (preferably 15 pounds cubed
   2 shallots
   ½ cup whole wheat bread crumbs
   1 zucchini, diced
   1 tablespoon basil
   3 apples, sliced

Directions.
   1.   Add ingredients, in order (spices last), into a pot, cook at 350 degrees Fahrenheit.
   2.   Stir.
   3.   Enjoy.

But please let cool, it can be very hot.

Source: Chef Marie Groufe

Birds.

Quelea Birds (Ujiri).

QUELEA BIRDS EAT ANNUAL grasses, seeds and grain. As soon as the sun comes up, they descend in huge flocks to find a suitable feeding place. After a successful search, they settle rapidly and can cause serious damage to crops. Flocks of red-billed quelea birds are capable of destroying entire fields of wheat, millet, and sorghum. Farmers use both conventional and unorthodox methods to kill this problem bird, these include methods such as the use of chemicals which may destroy the environment, bobby traps, and scarecrows. Environmentalists have sounded alarm bells as chemicals may affect other animal species and the environment. Commercial farmers in Zimbabwe export quelea birds' meat to France where they are processed and consumed as a delicacy. Quelea birds' meat is tasty and nutritious.

How to Prepare Quelea Birds

Zimbabweans use a simple and basic method for cooking the quelea birds. They do not use a lot of additives.

Ingredients.
> I kilogram of quelea.
> I large chopped tomato
> I large chopped onion
> I large chopped onion
> I teaspoon salt.

Method.
1. Remove quelea feathers physically.
2. Remove the innards using a sharp knife.
3. Boil the quelea birds for 30 -40 minutes.
4. When the meat is tender, and the water is almost done in the stock pot, fry the quelea birds' meat using cooking oil using a cooking stick for about 5 minutes.
5. Add the chopped onion and stir until the onion is brown.
6. Add the chopped tomatoes and cook for about 5 minutes and cook for about 5 minutes. Add a bit of water and salt for some soup and to taste and put a lead on the stock pot.
7. Leave to simmer on very low temperature for about 7 to 8 minutes.
8. Serve with "sadza." Or take to the market for sale.

Andrew Nyakupfuka

Ostrich.

The ostrich is a flightless bird native to Africa where it is found both on commercial farms and in the wild, however, ostriches are now found everywhere in the world as they are quite adaptable, for example ostriches are found in some very cold countries like Sweden. They look like the Emu of Australia and they share the same characteristics. Ostriches have long necks and legs, it is believed that their legs are so powerful that they can kick and trample a human being to death. Ostriches are reared on commercial farms for their meat, feathers, skins, and eggs. Ostrich meat and eggs are considered delicacies all over the world. Ostriches have red meat. Ostrich dark red meat tastes like lean beef meat and is low in fat and cholesterol, as well as high in calcium, protein and iron. Ostrich meat is regarded as a delicacy in Europe and America. Zimbabwe is one of the largest exporters of live ostriches and ostrich products.

Ostriches mainly feed on seeds and other plant matter; occasionally they also eat insects such as locusts, bugs, and crickets, beetles and many others. They do not have teeth hence they swallow their food without chewing. They swallow pebbles that help to grind the swallowed foods in the gizzard. It has been observed that ostriches can go for long periods without drinking water, they can make up with the moisture in the food they eat, and hence they can be found in some semi arid regions such as the Kalahari and Namib deserts in Botswana and Namibia respectively.However, it has been observed that they enjoy bathing whenever they come across some water. Ostriches have an acute eyesight and hearing for impending danger. They are threatened by such predators as lions, hyenas, and jackals, wild dogs and humans. Ostriches are oviparous which means the females lay their fertilized eggs in a single communal nest, or a simple pit scraped in the ground .The nest may contain fifteen to sixty eggs.

Ostrich is not only a delicacy but it has some luxurious by products which are marketed commercially. Ostrich skins or pelts can be used for making handbags, wallets, purses, and belts. Ostrich feathers are also used for making a diversity of the products for example; the white plume feathers are in great demand in the world of fashion and entertainment as well as table decorations at weddings and dinners. Small colored feathers are used as confetti at weddings. It has been observed that ostrich feathers are used to make ostrich pillow- pocket for a nap in the office provides a micro environment in which to take a warm and comfortable power nap at ease. It is neither a pillow nor a cushion, nor a bed, nor a garment, but a bit of each at the same time. Although ostrich eggs are a delicacy, ostrich empty egg shells can be used for artworks, engraving and decoupage. They can also be used in the manufacture of costume jewelry and even for making beautiful lamps.

Ostrich.

Ostrich (Mhou): It can run to maximum
of 65 kilometers an hour.
Photographer: Christiaan Kooyman.

Recipes

Karoo Roast Ostrich Steak.

Ingredients.
   2 ostrich steaks, thinly sliced
   1 onion, finely sliced
   100 ml cream
   250 ml white wine
   6 green peppercorns, lightly crushed
   100g mealie meal(ground maize)
   1 pumpkin, peeled and cubed
   200 ml red wine
   6 juniper berries, lightly crushed

Instructions
1. Slice the ostrich steaks as finely as you can and marinate in the red wine and juniper berries on the fridge over night.
2. Add the pumpkin and mealie meal to a pot, cover with water and boil for about 30 minutes, or until the pumpkin is hot.
3. Add more water if desired.
4. When cooked pour-off any excess liquid and mash the pumpkin and mealie meal together.
5. Meanwhile, add the onion to a pan and sweat in a little butter until just nut brown.
6. Add the cream, white wine and green peppercorns and bring to a gentle simmer.
7. Season and add a little arrowroot if the sauce is too thin for your taste.
8. Finally cook the ostrich by flash-frying the meat in a pan.

9. Do not over-cook as the meat will become very dry.
10. To serve place the pumpkin mash in the centre of a plate, arrange the strips of ostrich meat around the outside and drizzle the cream sauce over the top.

PAN-FRIED OSTRICH WITH CREAMY MUSHROOMS, BOMBAY SWEET POTATOES AND RED WINE SAUCE

Instructions

(a) For the ostrich
1 tablespoon olive oil
½ onion, chopped
1 clove garlic, chopped
175 g/6 oz ostrich fillet
Salt and freshly ground black pepper

(b) For the red wine sauce
125 ml/4 fl oz red wine
25g/1oz butter

(c) For the creamy mushrooms
Dash olive oil
100/31/2 oz mixed mushrooms, sliced
1 clove garlic, chopped
150/5fl oz double cream
2 teaspoon wholegrain mustard
Dash white wine
Salt and freshly ground black pepper

For the Bombay Potatoes
Dash olive oil
½ onion, chopped
1 clove garlic, chopped
1 sweet potato, cut into cubes
½ teaspoon cumin seeds
½ teaspoon paprika
Pinch chilli flakes

ANDREW NYAKUPFUKA

Salt and freshly ground black pepper
I tablespoon olive oil
½ onion, chopped
175g/6oz ostrich fillet
Water

Preparation method.
1. For the ostrich, heat the olive oil in a frying pan, add the onion and fry for 3-4 minutes, or until softened. Add the garlic and fry for one minute, then add the ostrich and fry until golden-brown on all sides. Remove the ostrich and set aside to rest for five minutes, and then slice.
2. For the red wine sauce, pour the red wine into the pan used for the ostrich, place over a high heat and simmer until the volume of liquid has reduced by half and thickened slightly. Add the butter and stir until well combined.
3. For the creamy mushrooms, heat the olive oil, add the sliced mushrooms and fry for 3-4 minutes or until turning golden-brown. Add the garlic and fry for one minute. Stir in the cream, mustard, white wine, and season with salt and freshly ground black pepper. Leave to simmer for 6-8 minutes, or until the liquid has reduced slightly.
4. For the Bombay potatoes, heat the olive oil in a frying pan and fry the onion until softened, then add the garlic and fry for one minute. Add the sweet potato, spices, salt and freshly ground black pepper and fry for 6-8 minutes or until the sweet potato is golden-brown and tender.
5. To serve, place the Bombay potatoes onto a serving plate, top with the creamy mushrooms and then the ostrich slices.
6. Drizzle over the red wine sauce and serve

Source.BBC .Phil Vickery.

Barbecued Ostrich Steaks.

Ingredients.
  3 cups tender ostrich meat cut into steak size slices
  1 tablespoon lemon juice
  2 tablespoons Dijon Mustard
  1 small onion sliced
  Salt and pepper

Method.
1. Tenderize meat with tenderizing hammer.
2. Dip meat into Lemon juice and rub with mustard.
3. Place in dish and layer meat with onions.
4. Let stand 2-4 hours.
5. Before meat is placed on the barbecue grill, remove from dish and sprinkle with salt and pepper.
6. Grill meat to your desire.

Ostrich egg with Tarragon and Pine nut tarator

Ingredients .
  1 ostrich egg
  2 tablespoon salted capers
  100g/ 31/2 oz pine nuts
  3 slices bread
  Bunch of tarragon, leaves chopped
  3 cloves garlic, finely chopped
  Maldon sea salt and freshly ground black pepper
  Rapeseed oil
  2 -3 tablespoon white wine vinegar
  Salad leaves tossed with lemon juice, oil and salt to serve

Preparation method.
1. Start by boiling the egg. Place it in a large pan of boiling water and cook for one hour topping up the water as necessary.
2. While the egg is cooking, thoroughly rinse the salt from the capers then soak in cold water for 30 minutes, giving them a gentle squeeze and changing the water every 10 minutes.
3. Toast the pine nuts in a dry frying pan over a medium heat until very light brown. Leave to cool.
4. Remove the crusts from the bread and using a food processor, blend into breadcrumbs, then transfer to a bowl. Coarsely chop the toasted pine nuts and add to the breadcrumbs.
5. Add the chopped tarragon to the mixture along with the

garlic. Finely chop the drained capers and stir into the mixture.

6. Season well with salt and freshly ground black pepper, then add enough oil to give a spooning consistency and mix well.

7. Finally, add a few tablespoons of white wine vinegar and mix once more. Set aside.

8. Remove the ostrich egg from the pan and place on a board. Carefully remove the shell and membrane, then cut into slices. Arrange on plates, add a large spoonful of the sauce and serve with dressed salad leaves.

Source: BBC FOOD
Oliver Rowe (Chef)

Pheasant.

Quail is the collective name for several mid-sized birds of the pheasant family. Modern quails are a hybrid of English; Japanese, and Mongolian, as well as Chinese pheasants. The males possess a plumage much showier than the females while the females have a plumage of more indefinite color, mixing dun and gray feathers. The ring-necked pheasant has a long history as a delicacy imported from Asia. Its tail is long and ends in top.

Pheasants are seed eaters that nest in the ground and are capable of short, rapid bursts of flight. The common quail was previously favored in French cooking, but the quail that makes it to our tables nowadays is most likely to be the domesticated Japanese quail, as this species is now bred throughout the world for culinary use. Ring neck pheasants are also hunted for sport and their meat.

Pheasants in Zimbabwe are of the indigenous type as there was no cross breeding. I hunted some pheasants known as "hwerekwere" in my vernacular language as a young boy. My friends and I used to compete in hunting pheasants in the fields and plains using catapults and retriever dogs. The dogs helped us sniff out the pheasants from the tall grass and crop stalks. We ate some of the pheasants and sold some. We could also give away some of the pheasants to the elderly people who could not hunt because of old age. The pheasant hunting competitions could also be between villages. There was no money involved in these competitions but self gratification. These competitions helped us get the best girls in the village because girls wanted good hunters who could provide them with food security. The competitions have since ceased because the pheasant population was depleted because their habitat was destroyed by the demand for land use such as farmland and house construction. However, some people in remote rural areas are still hunting pheasants for the pot. Pheasant hunting as a sport is no longer popular. Pheasant meat is regarded as a delicacy in Zimbabwe because of its scarcity. Those who can get hold of pheasants sell them for a very good price.

Pheasant Recipe.

Ingredients.
    1 pheasant, cut up into pieces.
    Soy Sauce.

Directions.
1. Cut pheasant into pieces and soak in soy sauce 10 minutes.
2. Grill over charcoals.

Smoked Pheasant.

Ingredients.

2 whole pheasant breast, skinned
3 tablespoons kosher salt
1 teaspoon dried parsley
3 pieces chicken skin, from leg quarters
1 teaspoon onion powder
½ teaspoon white pepper
1 quart cold water
1 teaspoon garlic powder
½ teaspoon paprika

Directions:

1. Dissolve the salt in the cold water to make the brine. Soak the pheasant in the brine overnight, but no more than eight hours. When the birds are finished brining, rinse them and dry them off with paper towels.

2. Mix up the spices and season the breasts lightly on all surfaces. Wrap the chicken skin over the pheasant so it's covered completely on top. You may have to play with the positioning a little. use one whole piece and one half piece of the leg quarter skins on each breast. When the skin is in place, secure it with toothpicks. Dust a little more of the spice mix onto the skin.

3. Use alder and apple for smoke -- these will give the pheasant a light smoky flavor.

4. Smoke for four to six hours at 200 degrees Fahrenheit, or until the temperature of the smoked pheasant reaches 165 degrees.

Source. Timothy J Higgins.

Biltong

The word biltong comes from Dutch with "bil" meaning buttock and "tong" meaning strip. Biltong in my language is called "chimukuyu"; it is popular with beer drinkers who eat it as a snack. It also goes well with "sadza".It is mostly cooked with peanut butter. Some people may add cayenne pepper. "Chimukuyu" does not require any additives such as spices or vinegar during the drying process; it is merely dried meat from any beef cut or game. It is a way of preserving access fresh meat because there are no deep freezers in my rural area." Chimukuyu" can be shared among friends.Biltong is a kind of cured meat that originated in South Africa. Many different types of meat are used to produce it, ranging from beef through game meats to fillets of ostrich from commercial farms. It is typically made from raw fillets of meat cut into strips following the grain of the muscle, or flat pieces sliced across the grain. Biltong is similar to beef jerky in that they are both spiced, dried meats, but differ in their typical ingredients, taste and production processes; in particular the main difference from jerky is that biltong is usually thicker and biltong does not have a sweet taste. Biltong's popularity as delicacy has spread to many other countries, notably Canada, the United Kingdom, and Australia, New Zealand, Zimbabwe, and the United States of America.

Biltong.

How to Prepare Biltong —Jerky (Chimikuyu).

1. Wash the meat.
2. Cut the meat at an angle with the grain into about one inch strips.
3. Sprinkle vinegar over the meat
4. Place the coriander in a bag and lightly crush the whole coriander so that the effect of the coriander will be greater.
5. Make the "biltong mix" by combining the course salt, brown sugar, coriander, black pepper.
6. Dip the meat into the "biltong mix" until all the mix is used up.
7. Place the meat in a tray for a few hours, or overnight, in the fridge.
8. After a few hours dump any blood that has seeped out of the meat.
9. Dip the biltong quickly into a water/vinegar mixture to remove surface salt.
10. Hang the biltong by making a very small incision through the slice of meat with a knife about an inch from the end of the meat.
11. Cut the string into about 10 inch strips which are placed through the meat and tied to form a loop.
12. Hang the biltong in a place not too far from an electrical outlet by taking the loop of string and place it on the hook or nail or hangar or whatever device you have created to suspend the meat.
13. To dry the meat, turn on the light(regular light bulb) and the fan and leave for about 4-7 days depending on humidity, temperature and taste.

ANDREW NYAKUPFUKA

Pangolin.

The Giant Pangolin is the largest of the scaly anteaters or 'pangolins'. It is primarily found in many African countries south of the Sahara desert and Asia particularly in China. Pangolins feed on ants and termites. Pangolins are considered a delicacy in many countries because of their scarcity. The giant pangolin has no teeth, it cannot chew. Its main threats are habitat destruction, the bush meat market, and the illegal medicine market. The giant pangolin is nocturnal. It is also a good climber and a good digger with its strong claws, which curl in its paws when walking around.

In Zimbabwe, the pangolin is a culturally significant animal, but ultimately persecuted and this is why it is listed as a "Specially Protected Species" in the country. Anyone who comes across a pangolin is considered a lucky person and highly respected socially. My father being a traditional hunter used to pick a lot of them. He used to surrender pangolins to a local chief. He was in turn given a piece of pangolin meat, a goat or cash for his effort. It is traditionally accepted that when you come across a pangolin you must capture it and present it to a chief. In so doing the, the pangolin's fate is doomed, as it is eaten and its body parts used in traditional medicine. The pangolin is only eaten by the chief and members of his clan. I have eaten pangolin meat because my father used to be given some pangolin meat by the chief as a reward. It is quite delicious and it tastes like chicken.

Pangolin body parts are used to treat some ailments in Asia and China in particular. It is believed that a pangolin fetus soup is used for increasing or enhancing men's virility. Pangolin scales mixed with herbs are used to treat a host of conditions such as masses in the abdomen, postpartum galactostatis, amenorrhea, and arthralgia, rheumatism, skin and external diseases as well as scrofula. It is further stated that pangolin scales are used to invigorate blood, promote menstruation, lactation, reduce swelling and dispel pus.

Pangolin Meat

Preparing Pangolin Dish.

Pangolin in Cumin Sauce.

Ingredients.
- 1 or 2 pounds of pangolin stew meat, cut into large bite —sized pieces
- 2 or 3 cloves of garlic, minced
- 2 onions, finely chopped
- Juice of 2 limes or lemons, and or a tablespoon of vinegar
- 1 chili pepper cleaned and chopped
- 3 or 4 tomatoes chopped (or canned tomatoes
- 2 cans of tomato paste
- 3 or 4 African Hot Sauce, or cayenne pepper or red pepper to taste.
- 3 to 4 teaspoons of cumin.
- Black pepper.
- Salt to taste.
- Several mint leaves (optional.)

Directions.
1. In a large pot, bring the meat to a boil in a inch of water. Cover and reduce heat.
2. While the meat is cooking, make a sauce by combining all the remaining ingredients in a separate pot.
3. Bring to a slow boil.
4. Turn off heat.
5. Add the sauce to the meat.
6. Simmer until meat is done.
7. Simmer some more.

8. Serve with *Baton de Manioc* (also called "Chikwangue") or "Fufu."

Shan Jia Chuan Xiong Angelica.

PANGOLIN STEW.

Ingredients.
120 grams of pangolin tender meat
5 grams Chuanxiong
5 grams of Angelica
Cooking wine
Salt to taste
Parsley

Directions.
1. Will Chuanxiong, Angelica wash.
2. Wash the pangolin meat and cut into small pieces and put into the pot.
3. Add Chuanxiong, parsley, wine, salt, placed in the fire, burning stamp,
4. Stir after boiling,
5. The fire to burn 3 Gaixiao hours,
6. Serve.

Leaves.

Pumpkin Leaves.

"Muriwo" is the general term Zimbabweans give to all leaves we cook and eat as relish while meat is called "usavi, or usayi". The leaves include the following vegetable types brocolli, spinach, and pumpkin leaves. However, Zimbabweans prefer the later as a form of relish albeit the dictates of a balanced diet. The pumpkin comes from the gourd family and one of its cousins is the squash. A pumpkin is classified as a fruit because a pumpkin is a fleshly plant that has seeds in it comes from a flower. Pumpkin leaves known as "mubowora" in my local language, are quite nutritious, containing iron, protein, calcium, vitamin A and vitamin C. The leaves are picked from the tips, which attach the leaves to the vine; otherwise the leaves would tear apart. The tips and leaves are sold together. We do not buy pumpkin leaves in my rural area as we grow a lot of pumpkin plants. Pumpkin leaves are a seasonal relish in Zimbabwe, mostly available in summer. I like pumpkin leaves mixed with zucchini flowers or young and tender zucchini fruit. If you buy pumpkin leaves you should keep the pumpkin tips attached to the leaves, as they are also edible. Pumpkin leaves may be available at your local ethnic, natural or whole foods store. Leaves may be used for salads, stir-fries, soups or as wraps for meat.

Zimbabweans eat pumpkin leaves especially urbanites who

do have not have enough land to grow a lot of the fruit making pumpkin leaves a delicacy. Several cultures in the world also consume pumpkin leaves just like Zimbabweans do. Zimbabweans also eat some dried pumpkin leaves. Dried pumpkin leaves are often cooked with peanut butter. In China pumpkin leaves are cooked and consumed as a vegetable or in soups. In Mexico and the United States of America pumpkin leaves are used to garnish dishes, they can be degraded to in a batter then fried in oil. In Kenya pumpkin leaves known as "seveve" are an ingredient of "mukimo." It is a traditional Kikuyu a mashed version of the Githeri- made of mashed maize and beans or mashed with potatoes or cooked bananas."

How to cook Pumpkin Leaves.

1. Wash and clean 15 to 20 dark green pumpkin leaves in water, using a new, clean sponge.
2. Remove any tough tips attached, scraping off the hairy skin if the hairs bother you; the tips attach the leaves to the vines and are generally cooked with the leaves.
3. Stack five leaves together, then roll them up.
4. Make one or two cuts perpendicular to the length of the rolled leaves, cutting straight through the leaves and placing the cut leaves in a medium bowl. Repeat with the remaining leaves and set aside.

Cooking Method.
1. Preheat a large soup pot on medium heat.
2. Add 2 tbsp. of vegetable oil or canola oil and heat for two minutes.
3. Sauté ½ medium yellow onion, chopped, in the oil for every 15 to 20 leaves you cook.

4. Add I clove of minced garlic to the pot and sauté for one minute.
5. Place the pumpkin leaves in the pot and cook till slightly wilted.
6. Sprinkle a ½ tsp. of salt, ¼ tsp. of ground black pepper, I tsp. of freshly grated ginger and 2 tsp. of fresh lemon juice over the pumpkin leaves.
7. Cook till the leaves and tips are completely soft then remove from the heat, or turn the heat to very low if you plan to add coconut milk.
8. Pour in just enough hot water to barely cover the leaves.
9. Add I can of thick coconut milk, then heat until the leaves are soft.
10. Taste the liquid in the pot, adding more salt, black pepper and lemon juice as needed.

Cooking Mukimo.

Ingredients.

500 grams potatoes
2 cups of green peas
1 green maize (soft)
2 bunches green pumpkin leaves
2 crated carrots
1 chopped onion
1 capsicum
1 liter vegetable stock cooking oil
4 garlic glove crushed salt
3 sliced tomatoes

Method.

1. Wash the selected peas and maize and boil for about 20 minutes
2. Peel the potatoes and wash them clean
3. In your cooking pan, heat the oil and then sauté onion and garlic together till golden brown
4. Add in the chopped capsicum, tomatoes and the grated carrots and stir for a minute then allow them to cook for about three minutes.
5. Add the chopped pumpkin leaves, stir and cover for another two minutes.
6. Take the potatoes and cut them into two parts and add to the pan, stir a little bit, add the vegetable stock and cover add some salt to taste and allow cooking.
7. When the potatoes are almost cooked add the peas maize and allow the mixture to simmer, reduce the heat.

8. Check to see if your potatoes are cooked after 8- 10 minutes.
9. If cooked drain out the remaining liquid till the food is dry.
10. Using a cooking stick (mugoti) mash the mixture until all the lumps of the potatoes are gone.
11. By now the mixture is so dry in the liquid we had strained until the food is of the right consistency.
12. It is good to make the food semi hard.
13. Garnish the food with a chopped coriander, serve hot with beef stew.

Source: Lillian Nikirote of Kenya.

Kenya Food Recipe:
Simple Recipe for Mukimo.

Green Pumpkin Leaves.
Zimbabwe way of cooking green pumpkin leaves.

Ingredients.
   2 pounds of pumpkin leaves, washed, deveined and chopped
   11/2 cups of peanuts or ¾ cup chunky peanut butter
   2 cups of water
   1 chopped onion
   1 chopped tomato
   1 teaspoon salt to taste

Directions.
1. Boil 2 pounds of pumpkin leaves in 2 cups of water for 5 minutes

2. Add one chopped onion and one chopped tomato
3. Process 1I/2 cups peanuts in a food processor until coarsely ground/ alternatively ¾ cup chunky peanut butter
4. Add to the pot and cook for another 15 minutes, stirring frequently
5. If the pumpkin leaves are too dry, add more water
6. When the pumpkin leaves are done
7. Drain excess water and stir in 2 tablespoons butter and one teaspoon of salt.
8. Serve with sadza.

Cow Peas Leaves.

Zimbabwean urbanites consider dried cowpeas leaves as a delicacy. Barrett (1987) says that cowpeas leaves are also eaten in different parts of the world such as tropical Asia, Attica, and humid parts of East Africa. Cowpeas are sown thickly and the entire plants are harvested in three weeks. The cowpea plant is known as "munyemba in Zimbabwe. Zimbabweans pluck out the tender leaves for drying and leave the plants to mature and eat the green pods or harvest the dry pods for seeds which they also cook and eat. The dried leaves are commonly known as "mufushwa" while others call them "mutsotso." Cow pea seeds are called "nyemba/ indumba." Boiled dry cowpea seeds are called "mutakura". "Mutakura" can be eaten as a snack or a relish. It tastes more or less like boiled dry beans.

Dry Cow pea seeds.

Recipes.

DRY COW PEA LEAVES.

Ingredients.
  500 g of tomatoes
  3 onions
  500 g of dried cowpeas leaves
  I cup of groundnuts (pounded or peanut butter
  Pepper

Instructions
1. Cook dried cowpea leaves until tender
2. Add chopped onions, tomatoes and groundnuts
3. Cook for 10 minutes, stirring continuously.
4. Add salt and pepper
5. Serve 2 -4 people.

ANDREW NYAKUPFUKA

Cowpeas and Rice Recipe

Ingredients.

 1 pound cowpeas (black-eyed peas)
 ½ pound salt pork, cubed
 1 large onion, minced
 2 x cloves garlic, chopped
 ½ pound cooked ham, cubed
 1x ham bone or possibly pig's foot
 Black pepper to taste
 ¼ teaspoon red pepper to taste
 Dash Tabasco sauce

Directions

1. Pick over peas for stones, rinse, and cover peas with cool water.
2. Bring to a boil, boil 1 minute, remove, and cover pan.
3. Let sit for 1 hour.
4. Sauté/fry salt pork till golden to release fat,
5. Add in onion and garlic, and sauté/fry till onion is somewhat softened.
6. Add in the pork and onion mix to the peas, along with the ham, ham bone, and seasonings, adding sufficient water to cover.
7. Bring to a simmer, cover, and simmer gently till peas are tender but not mashed, 1 to 2 hrs.
8. Taste for seasoning and adjust.
9. Cook rice separately. Mound rice on a platter and surround with peas.
10. Serves 6 to 8.

Hopping John Recipe

Ingredients.
- 1 cup Dry cow peas
- 4 cups water
- 1 medium onion, sliced
- ½ x bacon, thick sliced, cut in ½ -inch pieces
- 1 cup Raw long – grain rice
- 1 teaspoon salt
- Fresh ground black pepper to taste

Directions
1. This dish looks like a normal starch dish, but the name is intriguing. In the South it is served as often as you wish, but always on New Year's Day, in that case it is to bring you good luck. I am told which the children were so fond of this dish in the old days which they would hop about the kitchen waiting for it to cook, thus giving it the name.
2. It can be made with black-eyed peas, red lentils, or possibly dry field peas, but the remaining ingredients are always constant.
3. Put the peas and water in a 2-qt covered saucepan and bring to a boil.
4. Reduce to a simmer and cook the peas, covered, till just barely tender, about 1 hour 45 min. You will have to add in additional water during the cooking process. Watch which the peas don't dry out. Drain the peas, reserving the water, and return them to the kettle.
5. Sauté/fry the onion along with the bacon till the onion is clear. Add in to the pot along with the rice and 2-1/2 c. of the reserved liquid. Add in the seasonings. Cover and bring to a boil. Reduce heat and simmer for 15 min, covered.

Allow the dish to rest off the heat for 10 min before you lift the lid.

Weeds.

Cleome Gyandra (Nyevhe /Ulude).

IT IS QUITE NORMAL for my local people to collect some wild plants'
leaves or roots and cook them and eat them with "sadza" as relish.
The wild plants' leaves collected may include," nyevhe, or runi"
in my dialect while the Ndebele tribe call it "ulude."Some urban
Zimbabweans even experiment with hedge plants' leaves around
their houses. Matt Styslinger in his article," Spider Plant: A Hardy
and Nutritious African Native". says that Spider plant (Cleome
gynandra, also known as African cabbage, spider wisp, and cat's
whiskers ,is a wild green leafy vegetable that grows all over tropical
Africa, Asia, and the Americas. The African native cleome gynadra
is believed to have originated in Eastern Africa, in Ethiopia and
Somalia. It is not formally cultivated, but grows in the wild or in
poor rural communities particularly in the Kalahari and Namib
regions of Southern Africa. Young cleome gynandra leaves are
collected, cooked, and eaten like spinach. The spider plant is
cooked and eaten fresh. The cleome gynandra has a bitter taste
.Therefore careful cooking procedures should be strictly followed
to reduce the bitter taste. Leaves, stems, pods, and flowers may be
boiled in water or milk or fried in a pan with oil. The addition of
milk reduces the natural bitterness of the leaves. Another common
method to reduce the bitterness is to boil the leaves and discard
the water, and then add them to other ingredients in a stew or side

dish with other vegetables and spices. In East Africa, fresh leaves are used in mashed foods. Dried leaves are sometimes ground and mixed into weaning foods for babies. In Zambia, crushed groundnuts are often added to the spider plant dish to enhance flavor. Below are some selected recipes.

Recipe:

SPIDER PLANT WITH COCONUT MILK.

Ingredients.
   1 kilogram spider plant leaves
   1 medium onion
   ¼ liter water
   3 medium tomatoes
   1 teaspoon salt
   ¼ liter coconut milk

Preparation.
1. Harvest the young spider plant leaves including the stem tips then remove the leaf stalks.
2. Wash the leaves with clean water and cut into small pieces.
3. Place into a pot containing 1/4 liter of water, add 1 teaspoon of salt then vegetables and boil over a medium fire for 10 minutes.
4. Add 1/4 liter of dilute coconut milk and boil for 10 minutes.
5. When leaves are cooked, mash in pot and add oil (or cow fat).
6. Using a separate sufuria pot fry onions till brown, add

tomatoes then vegetables and 1/4 liter of thick coconut milk (or fresh cow's milk).

7. Cook for 5 minutes, stirring occasionally.
8. The above provides 4 to 6 medium portions.
9. It is best served with chapati, rice or ugali.
10. To mix with other vegetables, boil Amaranth leaves and spider plant separately.
11. When cooked, mix both then mash in one pot.

Amaranthus.

"Amaranthus caudatus" is a species of annual flowering plant. It is also known by different names for example, love-lies-bleeding, love-lies-a' bleeding, pendant amaranth, tassel flower, velvet flower, foxtail amaranth, and quilete. Zimbabweans call it "chowa, mowa, guru or imbuya" Most people in Zimbabwe do not eat "aramanthus" but those who eat it consider it to be a delicacy. Many parts of the plant, including the leaves and seeds, are edible, and are frequently used as a source of food in India and South America where it is called "kiwichi". Another species known as Palmer amaranth was once widely cultivated and eaten by Native Americans across North America, both for its abundant seeds and as a cooked or dried green vegetable.

It is documented that other related Amaranthus species have been grown as crops for their greens and seeds for thousands of years in Mexico, South America, the Caribbean, Africa, India, and China. The plant can be toxic to both livestock animals and humans due to the presence of nitrates in the leaves. Amaranthus has a tendency to absorb excess soil nitrogen, and if grown in overly fertilized soils, it can contain excessive levels of nitrates.

Amranthus Recipe.

AMARANTH (BASIC RECIPE)

Ingredients.
    11/2 cups of water
    11/2 cup amaranth
    Salt
    Water

Directions:
1. Combine water, the amaranth, and a pinch of salt in a small saucepan.
2. Bring to a boil, reduce the heat and simmer for about 25 minutes or until all the water is absorbed.
3. Serve like rice.

Source: Deborah Madison.

Amaranth Leaf Soup

Ingredients.

1 tablespoon butter

1 tablespoon olive oil

1 medium onion, diced

3 garlic cloves, minced

4 slices bacon, diced

1 big bunch (about 1 pound) amaranth leaves, stems removed
   and roughly chopped

¼ parsley

2 -3 cups chicken stock

½ cup crème fraiche, plus extra garnishing

Squeeze of lemon juice

Salt to taste

Pepper to taste

Directions.

1. Melt the butter in olive oil in a large pot or Dutch oven over medium heat.

2. Add the onion and cook about 5 minutes until softened.

3. Add the garlic and cook for another minute. Add the bacon and continue to cook another 5 minutes or so until the fat has rendered.

4. Add the amaranth leaves and parsley and cook, stirring frequently, until greens are wilted and tender.

5. Add 2 cups of stock to start (you can always add more later) and bring to a boil.

6. Lower the heat and simmer for about 10 minutes.

ANDREW NYAKUPFUKA

7. Transfer to a blender and puree until smooth (since the liquid is hot, puree in batches and hold down the top of the blender with a kitchen towel).
8. Return to pot and add more stock if it needs to be thinned out a little.
9. Stir in 1/2 cup crème fraiche and the squeeze of lemon juice. Taste and adjust seasoning.
10. Ladle into bowls and top with an extra dollop of crème fraiche.

Pasta with Amaranth Leaf Recipe

Ingredients.
- 1 pound whole wheat pasta shells
- 10 ounces Amaranth leaves
- 2 tablespoons olive oil
- 7 tablespoons cloves garlic, minced
- 1 teaspoon dried red pepper flakes
- Salt to taste
- Parmesan cheese, freshly grated, to taste

Directions.
1. Cook pasta according to package directions.
2. Drain and reserve.
3. Heat oil in a large skillet over medium heat.
4. Add Amaranth leaves, garlic, and red pepper flakes; sauté for 5 minutes or until the garlic turns light gold.
5. Add cooked pasta and mix well.
6. Season with salt and parmesan.
7. Serve.

Corchorus Olitorius.

My local people call corchorous olitorious," nyenje, bvunzwa, gusha or idelele in the Ndebele language. Women and girls collect the plants from the wild and pluck off the tender leaves at the end of the plants. The tender leaves can be cooked fresh using baking soda which we call "mutyora" as relish. There is no need to use stock oil, tomatoes or onions. Some of the corchorus olitorious leaves are sun dried to preserve them for future use particularly in spring. Some cultures use the seed for flavoring other dishes. The leaves are used as a herbal tea. Nutritionists have established that the leaves of Corchorus are rich in beta carotene, iron, and calcium, as well as vitamin C. Corchorus leaves are consumed in the cuisines in various countries for example in southern Asia, the Middle East, and Africa.Corchrous olitorious' cousin, the corchorus capsularis is consumed in Japan and China. Corchorus has a slimy texture, similar to okra, when cooked.

The young leaves of Corchorus species are known in Arabic as "malukhiyah" and are used as green leafy vegetables. "Malukhiyah" is eaten widely in Egypt and some consider it the Egyptian national dish. It recorded in some history books that the Corchorus olitorious was once a staple food in Egypt since the time of the Pharaohs. In Sierra Leone corchorus olitorious is known as "krain krain" and is cooked as stew. The stew is usually eaten with rice or "foofoo," a traditional food made from cassava.

Corchorus Olitorious (Nyenje/ Gusha/ Idelele.) Corchorus
Olitorius was once perceived as a national dish in Egypt.
Photographer: Francisco Manuel Blanco.

Corchorus Olitorious Recipes.

Mloukhia/ Chorchorous Olitorius.

Ingredients.
   4 chicken thighs and drumsticks
   700 – I kilogram of Mloukhia leaves
   10 cloves of garlic
   I tablespoon dried coriander
   Salt
   Pepper

Directions.
1.   Fry Chicken in its own fat until the skin in golden brown preferably in a cast iron skillet.
2.   Add half the garlic and fry until just turning color.
3.   Add a half a cup of water and the Mloukhia leaves and cook until wilted, mixing to bring fresh leaves to the bottom.
4.   Fry the rest of the garlic and coriander in oil until golden brown and pour over the Mloukhia. Serve over white rice.

Bidens Pilosa.

Bidens pilosa known as "Nhungimira, kanzota, or ucucuza" or blackjack in Zimbabwe is commonly known with a variety of names such as cobbler's pegs or Spanish needle or blackjack is an annual plant that grows in the wild. It may grow up to one meter depending on local climate conditions. The plant is considered a weed in some tropical habitats. In some parts of Zimbabwe like in Manicaland province the Biden Pilosa plant is considered a delicacy. Its tender shoots and young leaves are used fresh or dried as leaf vegetable particularly in times of scarcity. The leaves are consumed raw or cooked, they have resinous flavor. Some cultures add the Bidens pilosa leaves to salads or steam and add them to soups and stews, Biden Pilosa can also be dried for later use. It is a good source of iodine. The young shoot tips are used to make a tea. Biden pilosa leaves are consumed raw or cooked.

The Biden pilosa flowers have small heads on relatively long peduncles. The heads bear about four or five broad white petals of ray florets, surrounding a disk of tubular yellow florets. The fruits are slightly curved, stiff, rough black rods, with typically two to three stiff, heavily barbed awns at their ends. They have barbed awns which they use to catch onto animals or clothing as a means of seed disposal.

The Biden pilosa plant has some valuable medicinal properties for example; a juice made from the leaves is used to dress wounds and ulcers. A decoction of the leaves is anti-inflammatory and styptic. The whole plant is antirheumatic; it is also used in enemas to treat intestinal ailments. Substances isolated from the leaves are bactericidal and fungicidal; they are used in the treatment of thrush and Candida. Extracts of Bidens pilosa are used in southern Africa to cure malaria. The Manyika people in the eastern highlands of Zimbabwe retain the first water used for cooking Bidens pilosa foliage for later use as a medicinal drink to cure stomach and mouth ulcers, diarrhea, headaches and hangover. The Zulu in South Africa use a suspension of powdered leaves as an enema for abdominal problems. The Chinese use Biden pilosa as a treatment for; influenza, colds, and fever, sore throat, and acute appendicitis, acute infectious hepatitis, and gastroenteritis, dyspepsia, and rheumatism.

Recipes.

In Zimbabwe Biden pilosa leaves are boiled with peanut butter and eaten as a relish. In Africa it is eaten as a vegetable. It can also be fermented with rice to make "sake." "Sake" is an alcoholic beverage of Japanese origin that is made from fermented rice.

Edible Flowers.

Flowers do not mean much to most Zimbabweans particularly in traditional and conservative rural areas as they are in other western cultures. However, due to colonization they now mean a lot to some educated people and urbanites who have embraced some tenets of western culture in some occasions such as white weddings, birthdays, funerals and other western related functions such as "Mothers' Day", Valentine's Day and many others. It is therefore unthinkable for my local people to view flowers as a source of food or edible. However, I have noticed some Zimbabweans eating zucchini flowers in addition to the pumpkin leaves. Western and some Asian cultures consider some wild and domestic flowers as edible or use some of their constituents to flavor certain foods. Edible flowers are those flowers that can be consumed safely. Edible flowers may be preserved for future use by drying, freezing or steeping in oil. Flowers can be used to flavor some certain drinks, jellies, salads, soups, syrups and main dishes .Flower-flavored oils and vinegars are made by steeping edible flower petals in these liquids. For example candied flowers are crystallized using egg white and sugar as a preservative .Edible flowers include the pansies, thyme, and zucchini, chives, and cornflower, chicory, and thyme and many others.

Pansies.

The pansy is one of the oldest cultivated flowering plants. Pansy flowers are edible, and have a taste reminiscent of grapes and mint. Some other names for the cultivated flowers are ladies-delight and stepmother's flower. Wild pansies are also known as Johnny-jump-up and love-in-idleness.

Pansies Recipes.

SUGARED PANSIES.

Ingredients.
  Egg white from 1 large egg
  Fresh pansies, organically grown and stems removed
  Superfine sugar

Directions
1. In a small bowl, whisk together the egg white with 1/2 teaspoon water.
2. Using tweezers hold a pansy and lightly brush both sides of the petals to coat. Sprinkle with sugar, shaking to remove any excess sugar.
3. Let dry on a parchment paper-lined baking sheet until pansies feel crisp, about 8 hours. May be stored in an airtight container for up to 1 year.

Source. Martha Stewart.

Cook's Note.
Raw eggs should not be used in food prepared for pregnant women, babies, young children, the elderly, or anyone whose health is compromised.

Zucchini Flower.

The zucchini (mangare) flower is a golden blossom on the end of each emergent zucchini. The female flower is found at end of each emergent zucchini .The male flower grows directly on the stem of the zucchini plant in the leaf axils (where leaf petiole meets stem), on a long stalk, and is slightly smaller than the female. Firm and fresh blossoms that are only slightly open are cooked to be eaten, with pistils removed from female flowers, and stamens removed from male flowers. Both flowers are often used to dress a meal or to garnish the cooked fruit. Zucchini is the only flower I have observed my local people eat.

You may stuff the blossoms with breadcrumbs and cheese, and then fry them in oil. For the best taste, pick the flowers when they have just bloomed, and remove the stamen and pistols from the center of the blossom. Wash them to remove any dirt or pollen, and then prepare the flowers to your liking.

Zucchini Flower Recipes.

FRIED ZUCCHINI FLOWERS.

Ingredients.
   Vegetable oil, for frying
   2 large egg yolks
   1 cup ice water
   1 cup all – purpose flour
   12 zucchini flowers with stems
   Kosher salt and freshly ground black pepper

Directions.
1. Pour 3 inches of oil in a deep fryer or large, heavy pot and heat to 375 degrees F.
2. In a deep mixing bowl, lightly beat the egg yolks and pour in the ice water; mix to combine.
3. Add the flour and continue to mix until the butter is the consistency of heavy cream.
4. Dip 2 zucchini flowers at a time in the butter to coat completely, letting the excess drip off.
5. Fry the flowers in the hot oil for 2 minutes until crisp and golden brown.
6. Drain the fried flowers on a plate lined with paper towels, season with salt and pepper while they are still hot.
7. Repeat with the remaining zucchini flowers.

Source: Recipe courtesy Tyler Florence and Joann Cianciulli.

Stuffed Zucchini Flowers.

Ingredients.

   20 zucchini flowers

   ¾ cup white rice

   1 tablespoon fine chopped mint leaves

   1 ounce onion, grated

   ¾ cup, plus 1 tablespoon olive oil

   1 ounce zucchini grated

   ½ cup fresh lemon juice

   2 pinch salt

   1 ounce tomato, grated

   2 pinches pepper

Directions.

1. Place the zucchini flowers in cold water to open and make the preparation easier.

2. In a large mixing bowl place the rice, all the chopped and grated ingredients, half of the olive oil and lemon juice, and a pinch of salt and pepper.

3. Mix well. With a small spoon, take small amounts of the stuffing and fill the zucchini flowers. Fold over the ends to seal the stuffing inside.

4. Place the flowers on the bottom of a large saucepan, with the openings facing the bottom.

5. Pour in enough water to cover. Add 1 pinch of salt, 1 pinch of pepper and the rest of the olive oil and lemon juice.

6. Cover and simmer gently for about 40 minutes until the rice has absorbed all the liquid.

Blue Cornflower.

Cornflower.

The cornflower is well known as the official flower of France. Wise Geek defines cornflowers as annual plants which are famous for the intensely rich blue color of their blossoms. It is believed that cornflowers originated from Asia and some parts in Eastern Europe. Cornflowers are mostly grown to the north of the equator. Cultivars produce cornflowers with some varieties of colors such as white, pink, and purple in addition to the famous blue. Cornflower blue is so distinctive that it appears as a color in sets of crayons and paints, and people's eyes are sometimes compared to cornflowers.

Cornflowers are often used as an ingredient in some tea blends and tisanes. They are famous in the Lady Grey blend of Twinings. Wild cornflower floral water is produced in Provence, France. It is obtained by steam distillation which can be used as a natural mild astringent and antiseptic to prevent eye infections as well as an alcohol-free natural toner.

Cornflower Recipes.

GORGEOUS GREY BLACK TEA.
An elegant blend that is lightly scented with quality bergamot, citrus flavors and cornflower petal flavors.

Ingredients.
Black Tea
Citrus peels
Bergamot flavoring
Cornflower petals

Directions.
1. Pre-heat a cup or teapot. Use 1 tsp per cup or 1 rounded tsp per person for a teapot.
2. Pour freshly boiled water over the leaves and infuse for 3-5 minutes.
3. Add milk or sweetener as desired.

Cactus.

I was surprised to see some cactus pads for sale in some Mexican food markets. I have never seen anyone eat cactus pads. Zimbabweans do not eat such pads. However, I was made to understand that cactus pads are consumed in some countries in North Africa. We only eat the prickly pears from the cactus plants. I am yet to eat cactus pads. I wish a friend can prepare and cook them for me. Edible cactus is also known as cactus pads. This vegetable is a popular delicacy in Mexico and some Central American countries, parts of Europe, the Middle East, and India as well as Australia. Some people speculate that its popularity is increasing in the United States though I have never seen people eat cactus pads in restaurants.

I am told that cactus pads have a soft but crunchy texture that also becomes a bit sticky when cooked, edible cactus tastes similar to a slightly tart green bean, asparagus, or green pepper. Nutritionists have confirmed that cactus pads contain the following nutrients beta carotene, iron, some B vitamins, and are a good source of both vitamin C and calcium. Cactus pads require some careful preparation such as de-spinening, trimming the "eyes," to remove any remaining prickers, and outside edges of the pads with a vegetable peeler. You need to trim off any dry or fibrous areas and rinse thoroughly to remove any stray prickers and sticky fluid. Edible cactus can be canned pickled or packed in water.Acitrones, candied nopales, packed in sugar syrup can be available in cans or jars.

Recipes:

SCRAMBLED EGGS ARIZONA STYLE

Ingredients.
    1 or 2 cactus
    8 eggs
    ¼ pound cheese
    Salt and pepper to taste

Directions.
1. Scrub cactus leaves and remove spines.
2. Use a potato peeler to cut around spiny nodules and remove.
3. Slice cactus leaves into bite-size pieces.
4. Saute cactus leaves in a small amount of butter for 5 minutes.
5. Remove.
6. Beat eggs in a mixing bowl and add shredded cheese and cooked cactus leaves.
7. Pour in heated skillet and scramble.
8. Serve warm.

Pork Stew with Nopales

Ingredients.

1 or 2 pads

2 pounds lean pork roast, cut into cubes

3 fresh jalapeno peppers

1 clove minced garlic

1 pound tomatoes

2 cups chicken stock

Salt and pepper to taste

2 cups water

Directions.

1. Simmer pork in salted water for 2 hours or until cooked and tender.

2. About 30 minutes before pork is finished add prepared" nopales" sliced into bite-size pieces. 3. Meanwhile, in a blender combine the garlic, jalapenos and some water.

3. Puree until smooth. Peel the tomatoes, remove seeds and chop.

4. In a large pot place the tomatoes, puree, pork and "nopales".

5. Add chicken stock and simmer for about 1 1/2 or 2 hours until tender.

6. Salt and pepper to taste.

"Jalea De Cacto "(Cactus Jelly)

Ingredients.
Prickly pears
3 cups sugar
½ cup lemon
6 ounces liquid fruit pitch
Boiling water
Cheesecloth

Instructions.
1. Place prickly pears in a large saucepan or kettle. Cover prickly pears with boiling water, allow standing for 2-3 minutes, and pouring off water. (This aids in softening stickers of prickly pears.)
2. Peel prickly pears, cut into pieces, and place in a medium-sized saucepan. Cover prickly pears with water and boil at high heat for 5 minutes.
3. Pour boiled mixture through cheesecloth. Drain as much juice as possible and discard seeds.
4. Measure juice. Combine 3 cups of cactus juice, sugar, and lemon juice in a large saucepan or kettle.
5. Bring mixture to a rolling boil. Reduce heat to medium-high, add liquid pectin, and cook mixture for 8-12 minutes, or until the mixture begins to thicken. Skim off any foam that may have formed.
6. Pour mixture into hot, sterilized, half-pint canning jars and seal according to manufacturer's directions.
7. Process jars immersed in a Boiling Water Bath for five minutes to seal the lids. Test seal when cooled.

Aloe.

The Aloe genus is native to most African countries such Zimbabwe, South Africa, and Madagascar as well as the Arabian Peninsula. Aloe store water in their enlarged fleshy leaves, stems, or roots. Aloe young shoots and flowers are considered a delicacy by the Zulu people, who cook and eat them. My fellow people do not consume the aloe. They use it as medication for treating wounds and chicken diseases.

Besides being a delicacy to the Zulu people in South Africa, the aloe has so many medicinal properties for example; the althea root powder has been used as a binding agent to hold other herbs together in making pills. Aloe Vera is the juice which is extracted from the leaves of the plant. It is rich in compounds like polysaccharides, mannans, anthraquinones and lectin, which are helpful in treating diabetes and elevating blood lipids in the human body. It also helps clean out the mucous in the body and regular intake of aloe vera juice prevents constipation. Buzzle: http://www.buzzle.com/articles/aloe-vera-recipes.html

Aloe (Zumbani): Aloe young shoots and flowers
are considered a delicacy by the Zulu people in
South Africa, who cook and eat them.
Photographer: Abu Shawka.

ANDREW NYAKUPFUKA

Aloe Vera Recipes:

Aloe Vera is a succulent plant with various health benefits associated with it. It is well-known for its medicinal properties, cooling and healing effects.

Poached Aloe Recipe

Ingredients.
 2 large aloe leaves peeled and cubed (about I pound)
 I cup sugar
 Juice of one lime

Directions.
1. Because the aloe is very slippery it is hard to peel, but it's important that you get all the fibrous green peel off the aloe as it is tough and bitter.
2. Chop the aloe into small cubes and add to a small saucepan along with the sugar and lime juice.
3. Cook the aloe over medium low heat until the liquid is no longer slimy and the cubes have the texture of resilient grapes.
4. Allow to cool and serve over plain yogurt.

Green Smoothie.

Ingredients.
  2 -4 oz aloe vera
  1 1/2 teaspoon maca
  1 tablespoon bee pollen
  1 teaspoon/ 2000mg vitamin C crystals with Rosehips
  1 -2 tablespoon glucosamine, chondrotin and MSM liquid

Directions
1. Blend all the ingredients and serve chilled.
2. You can also add variations to your smoothie by adding fruits like mango, pineapple, pear and banana.

Aloe Vera Orange Juice.

Ingredients.
  3 -5 oranges
  Aloe vera leaves
  Aloe vera leaves

Direction
1. Split the leaves into halves and scoop the gel from the center of the leaves.
2. In a blender, put the aloe vera gel and add oranges to it.
3. Blend the mixture for about 2-3 minutes and strain the juice.
4. Place the juice in the refrigerator for 2-3 hours and dilute the mixture with fruit juice or water. Serve chilled.

Source : Kanika Khara

Ryzhomes.

Coleus Esculenta.

Coleus esculenta is indigenous to Africa, where it is grown for its edible tubers. It is also known by the following names, "dazo, rizga, umbondive", finger potato, and Livingstone potato. Zimbabweans also call it by different names such as "tsenza, shezha, mubvumbe or tsaya."The plants grow well in moist well-drained soil, and typically grow up to one meter tall. Some people grow coleus as ornamental plants. They are heat-tolerant, but they do less well in full sun in subtropical areas than in the shade. Zimbabweans grow coleus esculenta as a seasonal delicacy or food in the same way they grow white potatoes.

Coleus esculanta has been used in India since ancient times to treat all kinds of disorders including digestive problems like abdominal bloating and flatulence, to alleviate all kinds of problems and discomfort in the abdominal area. The plant has also been used in the treatment of vaginal and urinary infections arising as a result of pathogenic infection.

Recipes.

Clean the coleus esculant tubers and eat them raw or boiled.

Ginger.

Ginger is a root rhizome with a mild taste which can be used both as a delicacy and medicine. It is generally used as a spice, or ingredient to flavor certain foods considered delicacies in certain cultures for example turmeric and cardamom. Some cultures consume ginger root as a delicacy. Ginger produces a hot, fragrant kitchen spice. It can also be pickled in vinegar or sherry as a snack or just cooked as an ingredient in many dishes. Ginger can be steeped in boiling water to make ginger tea. Ginger can also be made into candy and ginger wine.

Some cultures use ginger powder in certain food preparations, particularly for pregnant or nursing women, the most popular one being "katlu" which is a mixture of gum resin, ghee, nuts, and sugar. In Bangladesh, ginger is finely chopped or ground into a paste to use as a base for chicken and meat dishes alongside onion and garlic. In Western cuisine, ginger is traditionally used mainly in sweet foods such as ginger ale, gingerbread, and ginger snaps, ginger biscuits and "speculaas". A ginger-flavored liqueur called Canton is produced in France. Green ginger wine is a ginger-flavored wine produced in the United Kingdom, traditionally sold in a green glass bottle. Ginger is also used as a spice added to hot coffee and tea.

Ginger can also be used as perfumery and a remedy for common colds and flu for example in the Congo where ginger is considered a panacea. Indians use ginger as a paste to the temples to relieve headache or consumed when suffering from the common cold. Ginger with lemon and black salt is also used for nausea treatment. Indonesia, ginger is used as herbal preparation to reduce fatigue, reducing high blood pressure, prevent and cure rheumatism and control poor dietary habits.

However, it has been established that allergic reactions to ginger generally result in a rash, and although generally recognized as safe, ginger can cause heartburn, bloating, gas, belching and nausea. It is also believed that unchewed fresh ginger may result in intestinal blockage, and individuals who have had ulcers, inflammatory bowel disease or blocked intestines may react badly to large quantities of fresh ginger. Ginger can also adversely affect individuals with gallstones .There are also suggestions that ginger may affect blood pressure, clotting, and heart rhythms. Therefore ginger may not be a panacea to all our ailments.

Mushrooms.

Edible mushrooms are the fleshy and edible fruit bodies of several species of fungi such as truffle, shiitake, and matsutake, portobello, crimini, agaricus and oyster. They can appear either underground or above ground where they may be picked by hand. Wild mushrooms must be picked up for consumption with great care and expertise as some mushrooms are poisonous to humans. Edible mushrooms are consumed by humans as comestibles for their nutritional value and they are occasionally consumed for their supposed medicinal value. People from my rural area of residence do not have any scientific technology to identify safe from poisonous mushrooms. They use some crude ways of identifying safe mushrooms. For example if they see baboons or millipedes eating a certain species of mushroom, they may pick up such mushroom for their consumption or for sale. There is no guarantee as to the safety of such mushroom.

However, some edible mushrooms may cause allergic reactions in some individuals, and food poisoning. Deadly poisonous mushrooms that are frequently confused with edible mushrooms and responsible for many fatal poisonings include several species of the "Amanita" genus. Zimbabwe urbanites consider mushrooms as a delicacy while rural folks view mushrooms as a good substitute for meat. Some rural folks have picked up and eaten some poisonous mushroom and died, for example the Herald in Zimbabwe (02/26/2012) reported that wild mushrooms account for a large number of food poisoning fatalities the world over, a development related to the morphology of fungi that makes it almost impossible to distinguish between edible and toxic species. They carried a tragic story of six people drawn from two families who died after eating wild mushrooms picked up from a bushy area close to their homesteads at Keryboom and Albion farms in Beatrice near Harare. Commercially grown mushrooms in Zimbabwe are safe but the price is rather prohibitive. Therefore most people resort to wild mushrooms.

Mushroom extracts can be used or studied as possible treatments for diseases such as cardiovascular, anticancer, and antiviral, antibacterial, and anti - parasitic, anti-inflammatory, and anti- diabetics properties.

Mushroom Recipes.

HOMEMADE CREAM OF MUSHROOM SOUP RECIPE

Ingredients.
   2 tablespoons butter
   1 medium onion, chopped small
   1 pound white mushrooms, chopped small
   1 clove garlic, minced
   1 teaspoon fresh thyme, finely chopped
   2 quarts vegetable stock
   2 cups heavy cream
   Salt pepper to taste
   Parsley ,to garnish

Directions.
1. In a large sauce pot melt the butter over high heat, about 1 minute.
2. Add the onions and cook until translucent, about 5 minutes
3. Add the mushrooms and garlic and cook until fragrant, soft, and browned, about 10 minutes.
4. Next add the thyme and vegetable stock. Pour the mixture into a blender.
5. Blend on high until very smooth and no chunks remain.
6. Pour back into the pan and add the cream.
7. Season with salt and pepper and garnish with parsley.

GRILLED CAJUN MUSHROOMS RECIPE.

Ingredients.
   ½ cup of olive oil
   ¼ cup of balsamic
   Juice of half lime
   1 teaspoon of Cajun seasoning
   ½ teaspoon of black pepper
   8 oz of Crimini mushrooms, cleaned
   8 oz of oyster mushrooms, cleaned
   Wooden skewers soaked in water for one hour

Directions:
1. In large, non-reactive bowl, combine the olive oil, balsamic vinegar, lime juice, Cajun seasoning and black pepper.
2. Toss the mushrooms with the vinaigrette, then thread on skewers.
3. Prepare your grill and preheat to medium-high.
4. Grill the mushrooms on top rack, turning occasionally for 3 to 4 minutes or until the juices are beginning to be released and mushrooms are slightly charred.

Shoots.

Bamboo shoots.

It is common knowledge that bamboo shoots or bamboo sprouts are food to the red panda of Nepal, bamboo lemurs of Madagascar, and mountain gorillas in Africa, chimpanzees and elephants. However, some cultures particularly in south East Asia also eat bamboo shoots as food or as a delicacy. Bamboo shoots are mostly eaten in Japan, China, Taiwan, Nepal and Vietnam. Bamboo shoots are also used in numerous Asian dishes and broths. Bamboo shoots have an acrid flavor and should be sliced thin and boiled in a large volume of water several times. The shoots of some species contain toxins that need to be leached or boiled out before they can be eaten safely .The sliced bamboo is only edible after boiling.

Bamboo shoots may be sold in various processed shapes, and are available in fresh, dried, and canned versions. In Nepal, a delicacy popular across ethnic boundaries consists of bamboo shoots fermented with turmeric and oil, and cooked with potatoes into a dish that usually accompanies rice. In Indonesia, bamboo shoots are sliced thin and then boiled with "santan" (thick coconut milk) and spices to make a dish called "gulai rebung". Pickled bamboo, used as a condiment, may also be made from the pith of the young shoots.

Bamboo is used in Chinese medicine for treating infections

and healing. In general terms, prepared bamboo leaves and shoots act as stimulants, aromatics, and work as a general tonic. They are useful in counteracting spasmodic disorders (spasms, fits), and in stopping infection and bleeding, stomach disorders and diarrhea. Bamboo shoot decoction is also commonly used for a number of female disorders: mixed with palm jaggery (tad-ka-gun), can be given once or twice a day for a week to cause abortion during the first month of pregnancy, used in the last month of pregnancy to induce labor, and following childbirth, eases in the expulsion of the placenta while preventing excessive blood loss.

Bamboo Shoots Recipes.

BAMBOO SHOOTS WITH CHICKEN RECIPES

Ingredients.

    4 table spoon sugar
    ½ teaspoon salt
    I pound cooked chicken breast, cut in bite – size pieces
    6 large shrimp, cleaned, cooked in salted water, shelled and
        deveined
    I cup oyster sauce
    5 tablespoons sake or dry wine
    6 fresh mushrooms
    I tablespoon soy sauce
    I pound parboiled bamboo shoots

Directions

1. Place shrimp, oyster sauce, sugar and salt in small pan.
2. Bring to a boil and cook for 5 minutes.
3. Boil peas in salted water until just tender; drain and add to pan.
4. Reduce heat to simmer. Add chicken, sake (wine) and soy sauce.
5. Stir to combine all ingredients well.
6. Add bamboo shoots and mushrooms and heat thoroughly.
7. Serve with your favorite rice.

Spinach with Bamboo Shoots.

Ingredients.
   I pound fresh spinach
   ½ cup peanut, vegetable, or corn oil
   ¼ cup finely shredded bamboo shoots
   I tablespoon salt
   2 teaspoon sugar

Directions.
1. Wash spinach leaves thoroughly under cold running water, drain well.
2. Heat the oil in a wok or skillet. Using a medium-high flame, cook the bamboo shoots in the oil approximately 45 seconds, stirring constantly.
3. Add spinach and stir until wilted.
4. Add salt and sugar, and cook, stirring, about I 1/2 to 2 minutes longer.
5. Transfer to a hot platter, but do not add the liquid from the pan.

Fatisia Shoots.

Samia Mounts a long-time nutritionist and gourmet, in her contribution to the Korea Herald (04/06/2010) said that Fatsia is a member of the araliaceous tree family, which have thorns on their branches. The trees bloom in August, and the soft shoots that sprout in the spring are carefully gathered and sold at the market at a high price, partly because they are highly valued for their health benefits. Fatsia roots are silky, smooth, and are considered a wild delicacy, much loved by Korean health advocates and foodies.

Fatisa is considered an effective treatment diabetes, gastroenteric disorders, arteriosclerosis, and high blood pressure. It is also considered effective in enhancing kidney function. As mentioned above, fatisia is most commonly used for stress relief, to help clear the mind, and to allow one to sleep deeply.

Fatsia Recipe.

Follow the following instructions.

There are several ways of cooking fatsia shoots; however, Samia Mounts says that steaming is the best method from a nutritional standpoint, because you will not lose any of the valuable nutrients.

1. Sauté the shoots with olive oil and sesame oil, just to spice things up a bit and test the versatility of this interesting vegetable.
2. Use mixture of olive oil and sesame oil for flavoring, as well as nutritional value.
3. Olive oil is a healthy polyunsaturated fat and is beneficial to anyone's diet. The result will be a delicious, flavorful dish that packs a solid nutritional punch, with plenty of protein and good fats.

Alternatively you can use the following simpler this fresher, more traditionally Korean way of cooking this fabulous veggie. All you need is:

1.300 grams fatsia shoots (dureup)
2.Korean hot pepper paste for dipping.

Instructions:

1. Rinse shoots with cold water.
2. Peel excess hard leaves at the root. Rinse again and dry.
3. Cut shoots in half lengthwise.
4. Steam for 5 minutes and remove to colander.
5. Rinse in cold water to stop cooking.
6. Serve with hot pepper paste.

Source. Samia Mounts.

Sumac Shoots.

There is a variety of sumac plants the world over. However, Sam Thayer Bruce in his article, "Sumac, The wild lemonade berry," says staghorn sumacs (Rhus Typhina) are shrubs and small trees that can reach a height of about one meter to ten meters. They are found mostly in rural North America landscape. Their leaves are spirally arranged, the flowers are in dense panicles or spikes. Each flower is very small, greenish, creamy white or red, with five petals. Sumac fruits form dense clusters of reddish drupes called sumac bobs. The dried drupes of some species are ground to produce a tangy purple spice. Bruce went on to say that the red-berried sumacs are used to brew a tart and refreshing drink (lemonade). This drink is delicious, easy to prepare, the fruits are fun to gather, nutritious, unique-and free. Its source is easily accessible to millions of Americans every summer.

Young sumac shoots are edible; they can be peeled and eaten raw. First year shoots of old stumps are the best, but the spring-time tips of old branches are also edible but not as good. You have to look at the end of a shoot after you break it off. If you see pith, an off-white core, it is too old. Break off that part then look again. You need a shoot stem that is all green. Then strip off the leaves and peel the shoot. You can eat it raw or cooked. They are very purfume-ish and slightly astringent. The sumac shoots should be eaten with caution due to possible toxicity. The bark has been eaten as a delicacy by children. The root should also be peeled and eaten raw.

The sumac leaves are rich in tannin. They can be collected as they fall in the autumn and used as a brown dye or as a mordant. The twigs and root are also rich in tannin. A black and a red dye are obtained from the fruit. A black dye is obtained from the leaves, bark and roots. An orange or yellow dye is obtained from the roots harvested in spring. A light yellow dye is obtained from the pulp of the stems.

Apes.

The term Apes may include such animals as the chimpanzee, gorilla, gibbon, and orangutan. The word ape can be synonymously used for a monkey. Gorilla meat is regarded as a delicacy by many countries especially in the equatorial regions of Africa which include countries like Rwanda, Uganda, and Cameroon, Congo Brazzaville, and the Democratic Republic of Congo. The gorilla is being driven into extinction by wealthy patrons worldwide who are prepared to pay ridiculous sums for gorilla meat.

Chimpanzee.

The common chimpanzee is covered in coarse black hair, but has a bare face, fingers, and toes, palms of the hands and soles of the feet. The common chimpanzees are social animals living in groups which range in size from 15 to 150 members. The chimpanzees live in a male-dominated, strict hierarchy, which means disputes can generally be settled without the need for violence. The biggest threats to the common chimpanzee are habitat destruction, poaching and disease. Chimpanzee habitats have been limited by deforestation in both West and Central Africa. The chimpanzee is hunted and poached for its meat which is considered a delicacy by wealthy people around the world.

Most people do not publicly admit that they eat chimpanzee meat. However, Claire Ellicot (2011) in her Mail Online article reported that Chimpanzee meat was on sale in Britain in lucrative black market, in restaurants, and market stalls. The meat, which can cost more than £20 a kilogram, was part of a lucrative black market trade that experts described as 'rife' in Europe. Trading standards officials uncovered the illegal bush meat from the endangered species whilst testing samples believed to be seized from vendors in the Midlands. Bush meat is sold not only in local African villages but internationally, including here in the United States. Many consumers consider it a delicacy.

Baboons.

There are five different species of baboons; all of them live in Africa or Arabia. Baboons are some of the world's largest monkeys. Baboons generally prefer savanna and other semi-arid habitats, though a few live in tropical forests. Baboons are omnivores fond of crops, fruits, and grasses, seeds, and bark, as well as roots. It is believed that baboons also have a taste for meat. They eat birds, rodents, and even the young of larger mammals, such as antelopes and sheep.

The majority of Zimbabweans do not eat monkey or baboon meat except for the elderly and the very young that may not care about the stigma associated with baboons. Some people do not eat baboon and monkey meat because of their physical likeness to humans. However, some Zimbabweans do not eat baboon or monkey meat on cultural reasons. Those whose totem is "Soko/ Ncube) do not eat baboon /monkey meat. It is taboo for such people to eat monkey. It is believed that if they do they will lose their teeth. Alternatively, they may get some bad spells in their lives. For example they may lose most their wealth through unexplained reasons. Their children may not marry. It is believed that baboons may come and destroy all their crops. The bad spell can only be expelled through paying a fine to the spirit mediums or the chief in their local area of residence. To be on the safe side they should pay the fine to the ancestral spirit medium (mhondoro) of the local district. The fine could be in the form of cash, some pieces of black and white clothes and snuff. Some people are experimenting with both monkey and baboon meat due to the scarcity of the traditional red meat such as beef. Zimbabweans who eat baboon and monkey meat say it is tasty and delicious. They say that the hands and feet are a delicacy out of this world. Baboon meat is generally used to feed park carnivores such as lions, leopards, dogs or crocodiles.

Some cultures consider monkey/baboon meat as a delicacy relished in stews, dried form and gravy based dishes. Baboon meat is particularly consumed in China, Indonesia and Africa. Monkey meat is considered as a good source of nutrition. Scientists in China are said to consume this meat in order to derive its health benefits. The meat of a monkey is amazingly rich in proteins which are needed for healthy functioning of body. The ancient tribes of Africa and South America are said to have survived for years on monkey meat.

Some people in Africa have stopped eating baboon meat because of the Human Immunodeficiency Virus /Acquired Immunodeficiency Syndrome (HIV/AIDS) stigma attached to baboons and monkeys. There is an unsubstantiated theory that baboons and monkeys carry the HIV/AIDS virus. Therefore most people have stopped eating baboon and monkey meat. However, like I said earlier own very few people in Zimbabwe eat baboon /monkey meat the stigma associated with monkey meat is immaterial. Zimbabweans believe that HIV/AIDS is primarily caused by promiscuity.

Method of Cooking Monkey Meat

The meat of monkey is usually made into dishes in rural areas of Africa. The meat is however preserved by smoking and is sold in the city markets. The fresh monkey meat is usually prepared in a spicy sauce made of tomatoes, chili peppers and onions. The smoked monkey meat is first soaked in water, then rinsed and finally drained. The meat is combined with sauce and prepared by simmering. Hot palm oil is used for preparing monkey meat and it is seasoned with salt and pepper.

Baboon/ Monkey Meat Recipes.

MONKEY MEAT STEW.

Ingredients.
   2 tablespoons onion powder
   4 potatoes cut into medium pieces
   2 small (8 oz.) of tomato sauce
   2 small (6 oz.) cans of tomato paste
   2 pounds ground chuck monkey meat
   2 teaspoons salt
   4 cups water
   Cooking oil

Directions.
1. In a 5 qt. Dutch oven (or larger stock pot), brown ground monkey meat then drain off grease.
2. In the same pot, add back the ground beef and the tomato sauce, tomato paste, salt, onion powder and 4 cups of water.
3. Heat to a simmer boil. (Using medium heat)

4. Add the potatoes and cook covered on low-med for 1 ½ to 2 hours until the potatoes are done
5. Stir occasionally.

Source: Donman Hammond, LA

SMOKED MONKEY MEAT.

Ingredients.
Tomato or peanut sauce
2 tomatoes
1 onion
Chili pepper
Palm oil

Directions.
1. Soak the smoked monkey meat in water.
2. Rinse and drain soaked smoked monkey meat.
3. Fry tomatoes, onion, chili pepper, and in hot palm oil.
4. Add tomato paste or peanut butter and smoked monkey meat.
5. Simmer until all is tender.
6. Season with salt and pepper.
7. serve with sadza or rice.

Monkey Feet and Hands.

Monkey Limbs (Zvirowadumba). Monkey feet and
hands are a delicacy to some Zimbabweans.
Photographer: Grez.

How to prepare Baboon limbs.

Remove all the fur/hair by burning on an open fire, the hand should be dried or smoked. Boil the hand first. When the hand is soft take it out and make some incisions using a sharp knife between the fingers through the palm to the wrist and let the hand clasp a tomato and an onion and tie the hand with string so that the tomato and onion are firmly in the palm. Cook the clasped hand/hands into a stew. Cooking oil is optional as the baboon hand has enough fat. This might take an hour or so. Once the hand is soft you can add a bit of salt, ground piri piri/ chilies or garlic. You can serve the stewed baboon hand with rapoko or sorghum "sadza" .Alternatively, you can boil the baboon hand for about an hour or so .When the hand is soft add some tomatoes, onion and peanut butter, let the hand and the ingredients boil for about ten to fifteen meats. The feet of a baboon are prepaered in the same way as the hands Use a cooking stick to stir. Simmer and serve. Some people eat the dried meat as a snack. You do not find baboon meat in Zimbawe's butcheries. It is only available from those who kill baboons such as game rangers who cull monkies and baboon.

Weird.

The Virgin Boy Eggs in China's Donyang City.

The recipe for Virgin Boy Eggs is quite simple. One first collects a bucket of piddle from the local primary school. Only the urine of boys under the age of ten is suitable. Virgin Boy Eggs are first soaked in a pot of urine, and then brought to a boil. Once firm, the eggs' shells are cracked to allow fuller penetration, and bathed regularly throughout the day with fresh piss to prevent them from overheating. People actively compete to obtain the widdle and street vendors can turn a tidy profit from selling them on the street. According to Chinese tradition, a VBE provides improved blood circulation, invigoration and even prevents heat stroke.

Source: In Life by Jeffery.

Cow-Urine Soft-drink.

Cory Doctorow (2003) in his delicacy contribution said that Radical Hindus in India are attempting to cleanse the nation of foreign soft-drinks by promoting an "ayurvedic" beverage made from cow urine: The bovine brew is in the final stages of development by the Cow Protection Department of the Ashtray Swayamsevak Sangh (RSS), India's biggest and oldest Hindu nationalist group, according to the man who makes it. Cow urine soft drink has some medicinal use for curing baldness, obesity, and constipation, irregular periods, hysteria, and cancer.

Om Prakash, the head of the department, said that the drink – called "gau jal", or "cow water" in Sanskrit was undergoing laboratory tests and would be launched very soon, maybe by the end of this year.oII

White Ant Eggs.

White ant eggs are commonly found and utilized as a delicacy in Thailand, Cambodia, and Vietnam. White ant eggs and scorpions gourmet are sold along the street stalls and restaurants of Bangkok. White ant or termites eggs soup are probably one of the weirdest choice out of the rest, but they taste surprisingly good. The soup comes with a mixture of eggs, half embryos and baby ants. The eggs are soft and pop gently in your mouth with a wee bit of sour taste.

Balut

Native to Philippines, Baluts are half-fertilized duck or chicken eggs boiled with its shell. It does not exactly look inviting as the semi-developed ducklings are already visibly formed. However, the Balut is a popular local dish eaten throughout the Philippines, believed to be an aphrodisiac and considered a high-protein and hearty snack. Often served with beer, the biggest challenge in trying out balut is overcoming its unappetizing sight, but most people would agree that it tastes much better than it looks.

Ha'kari.

Ha'kari is an Iceland fermented, dried Greenland or basking shark delicacy. The Greenland shark itself is poisonous when fresh due to a high content of urea and trim ethylamine oxide, but may be consumed after being processed. It has a particular ammonia smell, similar to many cleaning products. It is often served in cubes on toothpicks.This tasty treat is prepared by burying the beheaded and gutted shark in a hole in the ground for six to twelve weeks. Following this curing period, the shark is then cut into strips and hung to dry for several months. During this drying period a brown crust will develop, which is removed prior to cutting the shark into small pieces and serving. The modern method is just to press the shark's meat in a large drained plastic container.Unsurprisingly; the end result is a noxious to pretty much everyone on the planet aside from the Icelanders.

Stracotto d' asino.

Stracotto d' asino also known as horse or donkey meat is considered a delicacy in France and Italy. It is a major meat in only a few countries, notably in Central Asia and but it forms significant part of the culinary traditions of many others, from South America to Asia. Horse/ donkey meat is forbidden by Jewish dietary laws because horses and donkeys do not have cloven hooves and they are not ruminants. The top eight countries consume about 4.7 million horses a year. For the majority of mankind's early existence, wild horses were hunted as a source of protein. Horse meat has a slightly sweet and tender taste .Stracatto's taste has a bland reminiscent of beef and venison. Stracatto d' asino is also low in fat. Meat from younger horses tends to be lighter in color while older horses produce richer color and flavor. Stracatto d' asino can be used for making sandwiches or cold meals usually smoked and salted. Horse meat forms an ingredient in several traditional recipes of salami for example, cacciatore, Milanese, and Fegatelli or Genovese.

Recipe.

Stracotto d' asino (Donkey Stew)

Ingredients.
   1 kg donkey meat
   2 onions
   2 bay leaves
   2 juniper berries
   2 tablespoons tomato sauce
   Extra – olive oil, as needed
   2 garlic cloves
   ½ liter red wine.

Directions.
1. Cut the meat into chunks. Slice the garlic lengthwise and make incisions in the meat with a sharp knife and insert the garlic.
2. Put the butter and the vegetables which have been previously chopped together with the lard, into a sauce pan and sauté for a few minutes.
3. Add the meat and brown it, turning it frequently. Douse with a few ladlefuls of stock, made with a stock cube and tomato sauce.
4. Cover the sauce pan and cook the meat over a low heat, turning from time to time, adding a few ladlefuls of stock whenever necessary, until completely cooked.

5. Halfway through the cooking, season with salt and pepper. In order to obtain an excellent "strocatto," the heat must be very low and the meat should be cooked for at least four hours.

Casu Marzu.

Casu Marzu is a traditional Sardinian (Italy) sheep milk cheese, notable for containing live insect larvae. Casu marzu is created by leaving whole Pecorino cheeses outside with part of the rind removed to allow the eggs of the cheese fly "Piophila casei" to be laid in the cheese. A female "Piophila casei" can lay more than five hundred eggs at one time. The eggs hatch and the larvae begin to eat through the cheese. The acid from the maggots' digestive system breaks down the cheese's fats, making the texture of the cheese very soft; by the time it is ready for consumption; a typical casu marzu will contain thousands of these maggots.

When the cheese has fermented enough, it is often cut into thin strips and spread on moistened Sardinian flatbread, to be served with a strong red wine. Casu marzu is also believed to be an aphrodisiac by Sardinians. Because the larvae in the cheese can launch themselves for distances up to fifteen centimeters when disturbed, diners hold their hands above the sandwich to prevent the maggots from leaping. Those who do not wish to eat live maggots place the cheese in a sealed paper bag. The maggots, starved for oxygen, writhe and jump in the bag, creating a "pitter-patter" sound. When the sounds subside, the maggots are dead and the cheese can be eaten. However, Casu marzu is considered to be unsafe to eat by Sardinian health officials when the maggots in the cheese have died.

Breast Milk Cheese.

Simun Miriam, a New York University student, started her cheese project to challenge the idea of health, ethics, natural, biotechnology and basically every socially conditioned idea in our head. She was motivated to embark on the project by asking herself the following question.

If we reject all technologically modified food in favor of what is 'natural,' how far back to do we go? If we are determined to continue to enjoy our cheese, perhaps it is most natural, ethical and healthy to eat human cheese?

Simun found three nursing women willing to have their milk turned into cheese. She screened the milk for diseases, pasteurized it and learned the basics of cheese-making. She came up with three main varieties namely, West Side Funk, Midtown Smoke, and Wisconsin Chew. Midtown Smoke and West Side Funk were described as "creamy and just pure heaven," and Wisconsin Chew's taste apparently reflected the vegetable-filled diet of the woman who provided its milk. She also described Midtown Smoke as mild. She described Wisconsin Chew as a bland. Simun said that some people love it, and some people are gagging.

Breast Milk Cheese.

Ingredients.
   2 cups breast milk
   2 cups regular whole milk (from any animal)
   1 ½ teaspoon of active culture yogurt
   1/8 of a tablet of rennet
   1 teaspoon sea salt

Directions.
1. Heat the two milks together to at least 68 degrees F and then add the yogurt. Let stand covered at room temp for 6-8 hours.
2. Heat the milk again this time to 86 degrees F and add the rennet tablet. Stir thoroughly and then cover securely for about an hour. You want the curds to be firm not gel-like or soft. If they are still soft return to the pot and wait longer.
3. Once ready cut the mixture into ½ inch cubes within your pot.
4. Slowly raise the temperature on the pot while stirring to prevent clumping. A ricotta like cheese will result. If you want a soft cheese continue heating to 92 degrees F, for a hard cheese brings it up to 102.
5. The curds will now resemble scrambled eggs, strain them from their liquid using cheese cloth.
6. Place the curds in a bowl and mix with salt. The left over liquid from the above step is also consumable.
7. Place the mixture into a container to shape it surrounded by cheese cloth. The original breast milk cheese chef used

a Chinese take-out box with holes cut in it. Remember to place something below the container to catch escaping moisture. Something needs to be place on top of the mixture to put pressure on the curds.

8. Store in a cool place such as the fridge for 14 hours or so.
9. Remove and wrap again in fresh cloth. You must re-wrap the cheese each day until it remains dry.
10. Allow to sit for several weeks. Outer edge will turn brown. The longer cheese is left to sit the sharper it will become.

Source. Chef Daniel Angerer's Recipe for Breast Milk Cheese.

(Chef Daniel said that he has not yet tasted the cheese.)

Amphibian.

Frog legs are a delicacy in France as in some regions in Europe which include some parts of Portugal, Spain, Slovenia, Greece, and Italy. Frogs are also eaten in countries like China and the Far East. Indonesia is the largest exporter of frogs. Brazilians, Mexicans, and the Caribbean hunt wild frogs for food. Some southern regions of America also eat frog legs.

Zimbabweans do not eat frog meat; however, I understand that some very old people eat a certain type of a bull frog called "dzetse" in my local language. However, I have never witnessed them eating the frog. I am told that they are prepared to exchange their pricy cock for a bull frog. May be the young generations do not know what they are missing in the name of a delicacy. Jews and Moslems do not eat reptiles, frogs, and other amphibians on religious grounds. Jews view frog legs as none "kosher" food forbidden by Jewish dietary law as they are deemed unclean. Frog meat texture taste is a bland between chicken and fish. Below are some frog legs recipes.

Frog Leg Recipes.

Swike/Swikee

"Swikee or Swike" is a Chinese Indonesian frog leg dish. The dish can be served as soup, deep fried or stir fried frog legs. Originally a Chinese dish, this dish is popular in Indonesia.

"Swikee" is originated from "Hokkian" dialect (chicken), which is probably a euphemism to refer frogs as "water chicken". The main ingredient is frogs' legs mainly from green frogs with the condiments of garlic, ginger and fermented soy paste, salt, and pepper. Once it is served, fried garlic and chopped celery may be added. Swikee is usually served with plain white rice.

Frog Leg Recipes.

BUTTER FRAGRANCED FROG LEGS.

Ingredients.
   1 pound frog legs, rinsed and patted dry
   2 teaspoons white sugar
   2 teaspoons garlic salt
   ½ teaspoon black pepper
   Oil for deep frying
   1 egg beaten
   ¾ cup cornstarch or tapioca
   2 tablespoons butter
   2 teaspoons garlic, minced
   Salt to taste

Directions.
1. Place the frog legs into a bowl and sprinkle with a mixture of 2 teaspoons sugar, garlic salt, and black pepper. Toss until evenly coated, then set aside to marinate for 30 minutes.
2. Heat at least 2 inches of oil in a large, heavy pot to 350 degrees F (175 degrees C).
3. Mix the frog legs in the beaten egg to coat, and then drain off excess. Toss in cornstarch, and shake off excess. Fry

in hot oil until golden brown and cooked through; 4 to 5 minutes. Turn once to insure they cook evenly.

4. While the frog legs are cooking, melt butter in a small skillet over medium heat; stir in 2 teaspoons of minced garlic. Cook gently for about 3 minutes until the garlic softens, season with salt to taste.

5. When the frog legs have finished cooking, drain well on paper towels, and then place onto a serving dish. Pour garlic-butter sauce overtop; serve with dipping sauce. Rinse the frog's legs and pat dry; set aside. In a large re -sealable bag, combine the saltine cracker crumbs, flour, cornmeal, onion, salt and pepper. Shake to mix. In a shallow bowl, whisk together eggs and milk.

6. Heat the vegetable oil and peanut oil in a large skillet over medium-high heat. The oil should be about 1/2 inch deep.

7. Dip the frog's legs into the milk and egg, and then dip into the cracker mixture until evenly coated. Carefully place them in the hot oil. Cook until golden brown on each side, about 5 minutes per side. If the legs start to brown too quickly, reduce the heat to medium. Drain on paper towels before serving.

Fried Frog Legs.

Ingredients.

24 fog's legs, skin removed

1 (4 ounce) packet saltine crackers crushed

1 cup-all purpose flour

½ cup cornmeal

1 tablespoon ground pepper

1 teaspoon minced onion

2 eggs

½ cup milk

2 cups vegetable oil for frying

1 cup peanut oil for frying

Directions.

1. Rinse the frog's legs and pat dry; set aside. In a large reseal able bag, combine the saltine cracker crumbs, flour, cornmeal, onion, salt and pepper. Shake to mix. In a shallow bowl, whisk together eggs and milk.

2. Heat the vegetable oil and peanut oil in a large skillet over medium-high heat. The oil should be about 1/2 inch deep.

3. Dip the frog's legs into the milk and egg, and then dip into the cracker mixture until evenly coated. Carefully place them in the hot oil. Cook until golden brown on each side, about 5 minutes per side. If the legs start to brown too quickly, reduce the heat to medium. Drain on paper towels before serving

4. Heat the vegetable oil and peanut oil in a large skillet

over medium-high heat. The oil should be about 1/2 inch deep.

5. Dip the frog's legs into the milk and egg, then dip into the cracker mixture until evenly coated. Carefully place them in the hot oil. Cook until golden brown on each side, about 5 minutes per side. If the legs start to brown too quickly, reduce the heat to medium. Drain on paper towels before serving.

Giant Bullfrog.

Giant Bullfrog (Toad). Giant Bullfrog is considered a delicacy in communal lands in northern and eastern Namibia.

ANDREW NYAKUPFUKA

Most Africans do not eat frog meat or any other part of frog meat. However, the giant bullfrog is considered a delicacy in Namibia, but eating giant bullfrog risks temporary kidney failure or a burning sensation in the urethra. Professor Daniel O. Okeyo at the Faculty of Science and Technology, University of Fort Hare, South Africa reported that rural folks in northern and eastern Namibian eat the entire frog with the exception of the alimentary canal, which may be fed to dogs or poultry. He further said that a significant finding was that, the premature consumption of the giant bullfrog before croaking and breeding may cause a burning inflammation of the urethra (more like bilharzia) or some kind of temporary kidney failure. People are advised to wait eating the giant bullfrog until it starts croaking. Despite this caution people in some areas choose to eat frogs prematurely. However, when they do so very specific anti-poisoning preventative measures are usually taken. The Oshakati/Ongwediva people area prevent poisoning by lining their cooking pots with pieces of dry wood from a tree locally known as "Omuhongo" .Alternatively the Okambebe/Oshikanopoison prevention consists of cutting off the frog toes before cooking. It is not yet established how this works.

Giant Bullfrog Recipe.

CAJUN-FRIED BULLFROG LEGS.

Ingredients.
  12 pairs of bullfrog legs
  2 egg whites
  1 tablespoon DIY Cajun seasoning
  1 teaspoon cayenne pepper
  1 teaspoon lemon pepper
  1 teaspoon baking powder
  2 teaspoon cornstarch
  4 oz. fresh beer
  2 cups all – purpose flour
  1 cup yellow corn meal
  1 quart peanut oil

Instructions.
1. I. In a bowl, add the egg whites, your favorite Cajun seasoning, cayenne pepper, lemon pepper, salt, Tabasco sauce, baking powder and beer together and thoroughly mix. Next, dissolve 2 tsp. of cornstarch in a small amount of cold water and add it to the mixture. Again, blend all of the ingredients together. This will be used to coat the frog legs.
2. In a separate bowl, with a lid, mix 2 cups of all-purpose flour and 1 cup of yellow corn meal together. After dredging the frog legs in the beer batter, add them to the bowl of flour and cornmeal, close the lid, and shake until they are well coated on all sides. (A large Ziploc-type bag can also be used for this.)
3. Heat peanut oil (or other vegetable oil) to 365°F. and

fry the legs for about 3 - 4 minutes on each side (turning once), or until they have turned golden-brown.

4. Do not attempt to fry too many at one time because it will bring down the oil temperature.

Source: Jacques Gaspard.

Edible Worms.

THERE IS A VARIETY of marine worms which are found on the ocean floor namely, the tube worm shells, the giant tube worm, seashell, and the serpula, palolo, lug and spoon worms. The giant tube worms grow up to eight feet in length and have no mouth or gut. They depend on symbiotic bacteria that live inside them for their food. These bacteria convert the chemicals from the vents into food for the worm. When the worms are very tiny, they have a primitive mouth and gut through which the bacteria enter. As the worm grows older, the mouth and gut dais pear, trapping the bacteria inside. The worm's tube is composed of a tough, natural material called chitin.

Earthworms.

An earthworm is a tube-shaped, segmented animal that is commonly found living in the soil. Its digestive system runs straight through its body, it conducts respiration through the cuticle covering its skin, and it has a simple, closed blood circulatory system. Earthworms are a hermaphrodite that is; each individual carries both male and female sex organs. They do not have a skeleton, but an earthworm maintains its structure with fluid-filled chambers functioning like a hydro-skeleton.

Earthworms are only edible if you remove the toxins that can build up in their body first. This can be accomplished by having them crawl around in applesauce overnight. They will eat the applesauce and so the dirt, with possible impurities, will leave their systems. Worms are delicious and tasty creatures, and very pleasant to eat for those with poor digestion. They're also gaining popularity in the United States of America for their protein and low-fat value.

Make Edible Earthworms from Gelatin.

Directions.

I.   Boil the 2/3 cup of juice.

2.   Pour one packet of unflavored gelatin into a square or rectangular cake pan. Add the boiling juice and mix until the gelatin dissolves.

3.   Cool until the gelatin is warm. The gelatin shouldn't be setting, but it shouldn't be so hot it is uncomfortable or dangerous to touch.

4.   Have the children sink straws into the gelatin so the straws fill with the mixture. Set a butter knife on top of the straws if they float.

5.   Refrigerate three hours or until the gelatin is set. The longer the gelatin is refrigerated, the firmer the worms will become.

6.   Pull the gelatin-filled straws from the pan and set onto a cutting board or clean countertop so the straws are aiming away from you.

7.   Take a rolling pin and roll the straws from the end closest to you up to the other end of the straw. The worms should squeeze out of the straws.

8.   If desired, cut the worms in half.

9.   Optional: Make a "dirt cup" dessert. Fill a bowl with chocolate pudding. Sprinkle crushed chocolate cookies on top. Poke a gelatin worm or two into the "dirt." Chill until ready to serve.

Source. Susan Caplan (July 8, 2009).

Land Snails.

Land snails are mollusks because they have hard shells which protect their bodies. Land snails have shells that are right handed in coiling. Land snails leave a trail of slime or mucus when they move .This helps them to navigate on any surface. Land snails can actually climb trees or walls with great ease. The slime or mucus also keeps their bodies from drying out. Land snails are stone deaf; however they have a strong sense of smell which helps them find food. They have one or two feelers on their heads which help them find their way or avoid some obstacles or sense some danger, hence when you approach a land snail it rolls back into its hard shell Some people confuse land snails from slugs. Slugs do not have a hard shell. Land snails are hermaphrodite, that is they have both sexual gonads, when mating they produce both the egg and sperm.

Land snails are eaten in different parts of the world. They are considered a delicacy in French cuisine, where they are called "escargots" which means edible snails. They include Roman or Burgundy, Brown, and Garden, Turkish, and Agate. The Portuguese snail cuisine is called "carocos" which is normally served in some cheap restaurants. Land snails such as the zebra snails are also eaten in some parts of Africa particularly in Ghana, Nigeria and Cameroon. Land snails are called "nyamangoro" meaning slow boys because snails move slowly. Most people have a misconception that snails carry some harmful bacteria. That is not the case; snails should only be properly cooked. Some people cleanse land snails by first starving them for about three days so that they empty their guts of any dirt or harmful bacteria. They then feed them with flour and water for at least a week. Snails can be grilled or stewed with different mixtures of white wine, garlic, and piri - piri, oregano, coriander and parsley.

Snail Recipe.

SNAILS A LA PROVENCAL.

Ingredients.
    12 snails
    3 cloves garlic, finely minced
    ½ stick butter
    ¼ cup fresh Italian parsley, minced
    2 tablespoons chives or shallots, minced
    1/8 cup diced
    ½ cup cream

Instructions.
1. Sauté garlic (and shallot, if using) in butter for 2 minutes.
2. Add the snails, parsley and chive mixture and tomato.
3. Cook for 2 minutes.
4. Add the cream.
5. Simmer over lowest heat, stirring often, until volume is reduced by a third and has a thicker consistency.
6. Serve with a green baby salad by green baby greens and Vinaigrette.

Source: Cooks.com Recipe.

Vietnamese Fat Snail Fried with Sate.

Ingredients.
   1 kg fat snail
   5 stalks lemon grass
   1 slice of green pepper
   100 grams ginger
   1 tablespoon cooking oil
   1 tablespoon sate (The type use with seafood)
   1 tablespoon minced lemongrass
   1 teaspoon minced garlic
   1 tablespoon minced chili
   2 tablespoons cold water
   ½ teaspoon salt
   1 teaspoon sugar
   Flagrant knotweeds are eaten with fat snail
   Rice water

Instructions.
1. 1. Soak fat snail with rice water for 30 minutes
2. Clean with water, to dry.
3. Lemon grass is cut stump, wash, to smash them to pieces.
4. Add to the pot 1 cup of water, lemon and pepper horns
5. Boil fat snails in 5 minutes
6. Put out to dry.
7. Boil oil;
8. Add minced lemongrass, minced chili, minced garlic, satay salt, sugar and water.
9. Fry over medium heat for about 10 minutes.
10. Fat snail fried with sate served with flagrant knotweed.

Snails Stew (Gibraltar).

Ingredients.
   1 lb snail
   4 tablespoons olive oil
   4 garlic cloves
   1 large onion, chopped
   4 large tomatoes, chopped
   1 teaspoon ground red pepper
   2 ounces roasted almonds
   2 ounces walnuts
   2 slices fried bread
   500 ml wine
   Salt and pepper
   1 bunch chopped parsley
   1 bay leaf
   2 ounces pitted olives

Instructions.
1. Fry all the ingredients except the snails and wine.
2. Remove the bay leaf.
3. Add the wine and simmer for 5 minutes.
4. Boil the snails and throw away the water (alternatively use canned snails.)
5. Put all the fried ingredients in a blender.
6. Add the snails

Source: Jane Gib

Seafood.

Seafood can be referred to all edible aquatic animals and plants harvested from oceans, seas, rivers and any other forms of water bodies for human consumption. These foods may include all fish species, sea mammals such as the whale, and sea plants like sea weeds and all forms of algae, mollusks, and crustaceans. Some of them are considered delicacies because of their scarcity and high prices. However, crabs, lobsters, shrimps, and prawns are viewed as delicacies in the United States of America, Great Britain, France, China, Japan, Australia and many others, Most of them face extinction because of over harvesting or over fishing. For example the ivory king salmon fish is facing extinction. Crabs, lobsters, shrimps and prawns are now protected species because their numbers have been depleted through over harvesting.

Crab meat is considered a delicacy in many different parts of the world. Crabs are harvested in warm seasons.The Maryland blue crab is held in high esteem as a delicacy in the United States of America. Crab meat comes from different grades namely; lump, flake and claw meat. Lump meat comes from the crab's large body muscles, flake crab meat comes from the crab's cavity while claw meat comes from the fins and claws. Claw meat has a strong taste. It is generally believed that crab legs meat is the tastiest while the king crab of Alaska yields the most meat about six pounds of meat.

Some cultures do not eat only crab meat but crab roe. Crabs are cooked alive. You can actually select the crab you want to eat from the aquarium in a seafood outlet. Crab meat can also be pasteurized .Pasteurized crab meat is a very versatile seafood and can be used in cocktails, appetizers, salads and soups.Crab meat is prepared and eaten as dishes in several different ways all over the world for example, most Asians prefer "masala" crab which is a heavily spiced dish. Those in Eastern Asia eat crab roe. Americans particularly the residents of Chesapeake Bay enjoy their blue crab with Old Bay seasoning. The British go along with Cromer crab meat which is extracted and placed inside the hard shell.

However, crabs are not eaten in most African countries particularly those landlocked countries such as Zimbabwe, Botswana, and Rwanda. It is taboo to eat crabs in Zimbabweans. However, some Zimbabweans in the Diaspora eat crab meat. I am a good example; I really enjoy crab legs meat. It has an excellent taste and flavor. Crab meat is only found in elite hotels and restaurants in Zimbabwe. It is meant for resident foreigners and tourists.

Crab Recipes.

CRAB-STUFFED PUFF PASTRY.

Ingredients.
- 6 ounces) can lump crabmeat, drained
- 1 cup grated sharp cheddar cheese
- 1 teaspoon (Worcestershire sauce)
- ¼ cup finely diced celery
- 1 tablespoon Tabasco sauce or other hot pepper sauce
- ½ cup Miracle Whip
- 1 tablespoon minced onions
- 1 (8 count) package Pepperidge Farm puff pastry shells, baked according to directions and cooled

Directions.
1. Mix together and fill baked and cooled puff pastry shells.
2. Heat in 350°F oven until cheese melts and heated through.
3. Serve warm.

Source: Thelma.

CRAB BACKS.

Ingredients.

500 grams fresh crabmeat or 3(170) cans of crabmeat
4 tablespoons butter
1 large onion
2 teaspoons chopped chives
1 tablespoon Worcestershire sauce
1 pinch salt
¼ teaspoon fresh chili peppers, chopped very fine
½ green capsicums, chopped fine
½ red capsicums, chopped fine
1 cup breadcrumbs
8 crab shells, cleaned, boiled and dried

Directions.

1. Put butter in large skillet, sauté onion, chives, and capsicums.
2. Add crabmeat, Worcestershire sauce, and salt chili pepper.
3. Toss in pan over low heat, with wooden spoon.
4. Add bread crumbs, combining all ingredients in pan well.
5. Divide mixture onto the 8 empty crab backs.
6. Dot each crab back with butter.
7. Place under hot grill until golden brown.
8. Serve immediately.

CRAB STEW.

Ingredients.

 8 -10 medium to large crabs
 2 green plantain (cut into small pieces
 1 small pig's tail (cut off excess fat)
 1 large onion
 2 -3 teaspoons Lea and Perris sauce (10 -15 ml)
 1 teaspoon salt (5 ml)
 1 teaspoon pepper
 1 small round red Ricardo
 ½ teaspoon thyme (2 ml)
 ½ teaspoon any of your favorite seasoning (2 ml)
 2 – 3 plug garlic (crushes)
 1 -2 thick coconut milk.

Directions.
1. To kill crab, place it in hot boiling water.
2. Remove from water with wire or long spoon. Dis-joint legs from body and crush the large claws.
3. Add season.
4. Boil pigtail and green plantain until tender.
5. Meanwhile, grate coconut and squeeze (leave 2 tbsp milk for Matilda foot.
6. Add seasons to crab in boiling water.
7. Add Matilda foot to soup. Cook for another 15 – 20 minutes.
8. Lastly, add coconut milk and taste. Serve hot.

Source: Thelma.

       ANDREW NYAKUPFUKA

Lobster.

Lobster meat is among the most expensive seafood in many countries. Lobsters are invertebrates with a hard protective exoskeleton. Lobsters molt in order to grow, which leaves them vulnerable to predators. During the molting process, several species change color. Lobsters have ten walking legs; the front three pairs bear claws, the first of which are larger than the others. Lobster anatomy includes the cephalothorax which fuses the head and the thorax, both of which are covered by a chitinous carapace, and the abdomen. Because lobsters live in a murky environment at the bottom of the ocean, they mostly use their antennae as sensors. The lobster eye has a reflective structure above a convex retina. Lobsters have blue blood due to the presence of haemocyanin which contains copper.

Shrimps and Prawns.

Shrimp and prawns are important types of seafood that are consumed worldwide as a delicacy. The terms are often used interchangeably. In the United Kingdom and Australia, the word prawn is more common than shrimp; while the opposite is the case in North America. The term prawn is also loosely used to describe any large shrimp, such as king prawns, sometimes known as jumbo shrimp.

Shrimp: Shrimp is high in calcium and
protein but low in food energy.

Source. http://www.shrimp-magic.com/
shrimp-facts.html#ixzz2Bl4E6Gzl

Shrimp and Prawn Recipes.

SHRIMP SCAMPI.

Ingredients.
> 11/2 pounds of large shrimp (about 16 to24)
> 4 tablespoons minced garlic
> ¼ cup dry white wine
> 2 tablespoons, chopped fresh parsley
> 1/3 cup clarified butter
> 6 green onions, thinly sliced
> 2 tablespoons lemon juice, fresh if possible
> Salt and pepper to taste

Instructions.
1. Rinse shrimp and set aside.
2. Heat butter in large skillet over medium heat.
3. Cook garlic 1 or 2 minutes or until softened but not browned.
4. Add shrimp, green onions, wine and lemon juice; cook until shrimp are pink and firm, about 1 to 2 minutes on each side. Do not overcook.
5. Add chopped parsley and salt and pepper before serving.
6. Garnish with lemon slices and parsley sprigs if desired.
7. Serves four as a main dish or 8 as a first course.

By Diana Rattray.

SHRIMP DIP.

Ingredients.
  2 pounds shrimp
  24 ounces cream cheese
  I medium size onion
  Minced milk
  I tablespoon parsley
  Salt and pepper to taste
  1/8 teaspoon red pepper
  Lemon juice.

Instructions

1. Heat the softened cream cheese in the microwave oven for about 20 seconds on a high.
2. Place the cheese, which kept in the oven in a large frying pan, along with other ingredients, like lemon juice, onion, garlic etc.
3. Beat these ingredients until it becomes light and fluffy when you touch it.
4. Add the shrimp to the mixture and blend it slowly until it finally chopped
5. Serve along with chips or other kinds of food.

ANDREW NYAKUPFUKA

Curried Prawn Soup

Ingredients.

45 g (1I/2oz.) butter or margarine

I tablespoon curry powder

I shallot, finely chopped

I apple, peeled, quartered, cored and cut into dice

45g (1I/2oz.) flour

570 ml. (I pint) fish or vegetable stock

570 ml. (I pint) milk

350g -450 g (12 oz -I lb) cooked, peeled prawns

140 ml. (1/4 pint) natural yoghurt

Directions.

1. Melt the butter, add the curry powder and cook for I minute on HIGH.

2. Stir in the shallot and apple and cook for a further 2 minutes on HIGH.

3. Stir in the flour and when well blended pour on the stock. Stir well and cook for a further 4 minutes on HIGH, or until thickened.

4. Leave to cool. Pour into a food processor or blender and puree until smooth.

5. Add the milk and cook for I - 2 minutes on HIGH.

6. Add the prawns and leave to stand for 2 - 3 minutes before serving. Top with natural yoghurt.

Finger licking Prawn Recipe

Ingredients.
  A few strips of bacon
  250 of queen size prawns (0.55 lbs, 0.039 stone, 8.81 oz
  ½ lemon, juice extracted
  200 ml. sweet chili sauce (1/2 cup 5 tablespoons)
  100 ml. white wine (3/4) cup)
  30 ml. butter or margarine (2 tablespoons)
  Salt and pepper to taste.

Directions.
1. Clean the prawns.
2. Wrap the bacon around the whole prawn.
3. Place in a greased baking pan.
4. Mix the rest of the ingredients.
5. Pour over the prawns.
6. Bake for 50 minutes at 180 degrees C (360 deg F).
7. Serve with steamed rice, pasta and a fresh salad

Sea Urchins.

Sea urchins are found all over the world. They are found in such countries like Spain, Portugal, and New Zealand, Japan and South Korea, the United States of America, Chile and many more. Sea urchins or urchins are small, spiny, globular animals. The gonads of both male and female sea urchins, usually called sea urchin roe or corals, are culinary delicacies in many parts of the world. In Japan, sea urchin is known as "uni,"and its roe is served raw as "sashimi" or in "sushi", with soy sauce and "wasabi."In New Zealand, sea urchin known as "kina" in Maori is a delicacy, traditionally eaten raw. In countries like Spain, Greece, and Italy, France, and Portugal, "paracentrotus lividus" is often eaten raw, with lemon, and known as "ricci". It can also flavor omelets, scrambled eggs, and fish soup, mayonnaise, sauce for tartlets. In Chilean cuisine, it is served with raw lemon, onions, and olive oil.

Algae (Zerere).

It is now common knowledge that marine algae, or seaweeds, are the oldest members of the plant kingdom, extending back many hundreds of millions of years. They have little tissue differentiation, no true vascular tissue, no roots, stems, or leaves, and no flowers. Seaweed is highly nutritious, delicious, and can be cooked with pasta, put in salads and used in meat dishes. History has records that show that the Chinese considered algae a delicacy offered during sacrifices to their ancestors. My local folks on the hand do not consider algae a delicacy but use it as a shampoo. Scientists have proved that sea plants are the most nutrient-rich plants in the world. They have categorically stated that, every mineral you need is available in sea plants, so the algae health benefits are endless. It removes toxins from your body, enriches blood, and makes hair shine. Algae makes your brain sharp, skin will have a healthy glow. It will strengthen teeth and immune system, and prevents allergies and reduces aging. Lastly it gives you energy and stunts the growth of tumors. Algae can be chemically processed and used in cleaners, fertilizers, and pesticides, and as well as sewage treatment facilities.

Algae Recipe.

KALE WITH SEAWEED, SESAME AND GINGER RECIPE.

Ingredients.
   ½ cup dried arame sea vegetables (food –grade seaweed)
   Dark sesame oil, about 2tablespoons
   1 tablespoon peeled and minced ginger
   1 bunch kale
   1 tablespoon minced garlic
   2 tablespoons Liquid Aminos
   1 tablespoon Toasted sesame seeds

Directions.
1. Rinse the seaweed in water and let soak, covered in water for 5-7 minutes. Drain seaweed and place in a large bowl. Add 1 teaspoon of dark sesame oil and the minced ginger.
2. Prepare kale by soaking in water to loosen any dirt, rinsing thoroughly. Chop cross-wise into 1-inch by 2-inch pieces.
3. In a large covered skillet, uncover and heat 2 teaspoons of dark sesame oil on medium heat. Add garlic and gently sauté for one minute, until fragrant. Add the seaweed and ginger, gently cook for 1 minute. Remove seaweed/ginger/garlic from pan back to the bowl and set aside.
4. Heat 1 tablespoon sesame oil in the skillet. Add the chopped kale. Add 3 tablespoons of Braggs. Gently mix in the pan to coat the kale with the oil and Bragg. Cover; lower heat to low; let cook for 5-10 minutes or until kale is wilted - soft enough to eat easily, but not so soft as to be mushy. Remove cover and let cook a minute more to evaporate any excess moisture. Remove from heat. Mix in the kale

with the seaweed ginger mixture. Add more sesame oil and Braggs to taste. Garnish with toasted sesame seeds.

Simply Recipes:

Beverages.

Drink, or beverage, is a kind of liquid which is specifically prepared for human consumption. Beverages can be divided into various groups such as plain water, alcohol, non alcoholic drinks, soft drinks or soda (carbonated drinks), fruit or vegetable juices and hot drinks.

A non-alcoholic drink is one that contains little or no alcohol at all. This category includes low-alcohol beer, non-alcoholic wine, and apple cider if they contain less than 0.5% alcohol by volume.

Tea.

Tea was imported to Europe during the Portuguese expansion of the 16th century. It was first consumed as a luxury item on special occasions, such as religious festivals, wakes, and domestic work gatherings such as quilting. However, tea is still considered a delicacy in some cultures. It is believed that tea plants are native to East and South Asia, and probably originated around the meeting points of the lands of northeast India, north Burma and southwest China.

Scientists have proved that tea contains a large number of potentially bioactive chemicals, including flavinoids, amino acids, vitamins, caffeine and several polysaccharides. It has also been suggested that green and black tea may protect humans against cancer. However, the catechins found in green tea are thought to be more effective in preventing certain obesity-related cancers such as liver and colorectal while both green and black tea may protect against cardiovascular diseases.

Indian Beverages.

Beverages are mostly made with buttermilk in India, for example mango lassi ,mixed fruit, and lassi ,apple cocktail, and mango milkshake, ginger tea, cardamom tea , and masala tea. These beverages are very refreshing and considered delicacies.

GINGER TEA RECIPE.

Ingredients:
  11/4 cup water
  3/4 cup milk
  1 inch ginger chopped very fine
  2 tea bags or 2 tsp tea leaves
  Sugar to taste

Directions.
I. Place the water in a sauce pan and boil, add the rest of the ingredients and let them boil on medium heat until the tea becomes a nice rich brown. Serve the tea with some vegetable cutlets or "pakoras."

Kona Coffee.

Coffee comes in a wide range of varieties, but Kona coffee is a special delicacy. Kona coffee is a term that refers to coffee made from beans grown on Mount Hualalai and Mauna Loa which are in the Kona Districts of the Big Island of Hawaii. Kona coffee is difficult to grow and has specific growing requirements. It prefers sun in the morning, rain in the afternoon, and mild temperatures in the evening. These very specific conditions mean that it can only thrive under the best circumstances. Because of this, Kona coffee is classified as a premium variety by coffee enthusiasts.

Recipe.

Kona Coffee-tini

Ingredients

    2 shots blended vanilla macadamia iced coffee (recommended: Royal Kona)

    1 shot coconut rum (recommended: Bacardi)

    Ice

Directions

1. Combine iced coffee and rum in a cocktail shaker filled with ice. Shake vigorously until frost forms on shaker. Pour into chilled martini glass.

Other Foods.

Sushi

Sushi, meaning sour tasting is a Japanese food consisting of cooked vinegared rice combined with other ingredients usually raw fish or other seafood. Sushi varieties arise from fillings, toppings, condiments and preparation. Traditional versus contemporary methods of assembly may create very different results from very similar ingredients. Sushi was first developed in Southeast Asia possibly along what is now known as the Mekong River.

Sushi Recipes.

Sushi is Japanese food by tradition, but it is currently enjoyed by cultures around the world. In the last 20 years, Americans have taken a strong liking to the cuisine, and it can be found in both metropolitan and suburban neighborhoods with ease.

Ingredients.

10 large uncooked shrimp

1 cup cold water

2 tablespoons vinegar

2 cups cooked sushi rice

1 to2 tablespoons wasabi paste, to taste

Soy sauce, for dipping

Directions:

1. Bring a large pot of salted water to a boil. Skewer the shrimp from head to tail with toothpicks.
2. Add skewered shrimp to boiling water and cook 3 minutes; transfer to bowl of ice water to stop cooking.
3. When cooled, remove the shell and skewers from shrimp. Make a slit in the underside of the shrimp and cut through almost to the top but not completely. Remove the dark vein.
4. Moisten your hands with a mixture of cold water and vinegar. Take a 1 1/2 tablespoons of the sushi rice and form into a rectangular block about 2-inches long with rounded edges and sides.
5. Scoop up a tiny amount, about ¼ teaspoon, of wasabi paste with the tip of your finger and spread it on the inside of the shrimp.
6. Place the shaped rice on top of the wasabi and press gently. Press into the shrimp, but make sure it holds its shape.
7. Serve with soy sauce for dipping

Chicken

The chicken can be defined as a domesticated fowl. As one of the most common and widespread domestic animals with a population of more than 24 billion in 2003. There are more chickens in the world than any other species of bird. Humans keep chickens primarily as a source of food, consuming both their meat and their eggs. It is believed that humans first domesticated chickens of Indian origin for the purpose of cockfighting in Asia, Africa, and Europe. Because of its relatively low cost, chicken is one of the most used meats in the world. Nearly all parts of the bird can be used for food, and the meat can be cooked in many different ways. Since there is a great abundance of chicken all over world, chicken is not supposed to be a delicacy because of its abundance. However, chicken is a delicacy in some parts of the world because of the way some chicken dishes are prepared, for example the most popular chicken dishes include roasted chicken, fried chicken, and chicken soup, buffalo wings, and tandoori chicken, masala chicken ,butter chicken, and chicken and rice. Chicken is held in high esteem in Zimbabwe and other African countries. Chicken meat is offered to most the distinguished guests, at marriage ceremonies and other significant cultural rituals.

Masala Chicken.

Masala chicken is a dish of roasted chicken chunks in a spicy masala sauce. The sauce is usually creamy, spiced and orange-colored. Chicken masala has been said to be the most popular dish in British restaurants. The dish is believed to have originated, probably by accident with subsequent improvisations, in Punjab. Chicken masala is chicken, chunks of chicken marinated in spices and yogurt that is then baked in a tandoor oven, served in a masala and sauce. There is no standard recipe for chicken masala; a survey found that there are more than forty -eight different recipes; the only common ingredient was chicken.

Recipe.

Chicken Tikka Masala.

Ingredients.

Marinade and Chicken:

2 cups plain yogurt

2 tablespoons lemon juice

1 tablespoon cayenne pepper

1 tablespoon ground cumin

1 tablespoon minced fresh ginger

1 tablespoon ginger juice

2 teaspoons ground cinnamon

Salt

1 teaspoon white pepper

2 pounds chicken, breasts and thighs, diced small

Sauce:

2 tablespoons butter

2 tablespoons minced garlic

2 tablespoons jalapeno or Scotch bonnet pepper, seeded and finely diced

1 teaspoon ground cumin

1 teaspoon sea salt or kosher salt

1 teaspoon smoked paprika

2 cups tomato puree

1 cup heavy cream

1/2 cup sour cream

Chopped green onions and cilantro, for garnish

Special equipment: fourteen to sixteen 6-inch skewers

Directions.

1. For the marinade and chicken: In a bowl, blend the yogurt,

lemon juice, cayenne, cumin, gingers, cinnamon, salt as needed and pepper. Once well mixed, add the chicken and allow the meat to marinate for at least 30 minutes. Do not over marinate.

2. For the sauce: Melt the butter in a large heavy skillet over medium heat. Sauté the garlic and jalapeno for 1 minute. Season with cumin, salt and paprika. Stir in the tomato puree, heavy cream and sour cream. Simmer on low heat until the sauce thickens, about 20 minutes.

3. Prepare a grill to medium-high heat.

4. Thread the chicken on the skewers. Grill the chicken on the first side for 3 to 4 minutes, then flip and repeat cooking on the second side. Once cooked on the second side, brush both sides with the prepared sauce. Allow the sauce to warm and then serve, garnishing with greens of choice.

Tandoori.

Tandoori chicken meaning, Roasted Chicken) is a popular Bangladeshi, Indian and Pakistani dish consisting of roasted chicken prepared with yogurt and spices. Cayenne pepper, red chili powder are used to give it a fiery red color. A higher amount of turmeric produces an orange color. It is traditionally cooked at high temperatures in a tandoor (clay oven), but can also be prepared on a traditional barbecue grill.

Butter Chicken.

Butter chicken is part of Indian cuisine, popular in countries all over the world. The origins of butter chicken can be traced back to Britain, where chefs created a dish to suit the European palate. Butter chicken is believed to have been first introduced by one Moti Mahal, Daryaganj. It is usually served with naan, roti, and parathas, roomali roti or steamed rice.

Butter Chicken Recipe.

Butter Chicken - Murg Makhani.
1kg boneless chicken skin removed
Juice of 1 lime
Salt to taste
1 tsp red chili powder (adjust to suit your taste)
6 cloves
8-10 peppercorns
1" stick of cinnamon
2 bay leaves
8-10 almonds
Seeds from 3-4 pods of cardamom
1 cup fresh yoghurt (must not be sour)
3 tablespoons vegetable/canola/sunflower cooking oil
2 onions chopped
2 teaspoons garlic paste

Directions.
1. Mix the chicken, lime juice, salt and red chili powder in a large, non-metallic bowl. Cover and allow marinating for 1 hour.
2. Heat a flat pan or griddle on medium heat and gently roast (stirring frequently) the cloves, peppercorns, cinnamon,

bay leaves and almonds till they darken slightly. Cool and add the cardamom seeds. Now grind into a coarse powder in a clean, dry coffee grinder.

3. Mix the yoghurt, above whole spice powder (from previous step), coriander, and cumin and turmeric powders together and add them to the chicken. Allow to marinate for another hour.

4. Heat the oil in a deep pan on medium heat. When hot, add the onions. Fry till a pale golden brown in color and then add the ginger and garlic pastes. Fry for a minute.

5. Add only the chicken from the chicken-spice mix and fry till sealed (chicken will turn opaque and the flesh will go from pink to whitish in color).

6. Now add the tomato paste, chicken stock, "kasuri methi" and remaining part of the yogurt-spice mix to the chicken.

7. Cook till the chicken is tender and the gravy is reduced to half its original volume.

8. Melt the butter in another small pan and then pour it over the chicken.

9. Garnish with coriander leaves and serve with Naan and Kaali Daal.

10. Cover the dish immediately. Remove the cover just before serving, discard the foil bowl and charcoal and serve. The curry will be infused with a smoky flavor!

Trivia/Facts.

Match the following delicacies with the appropriate countries.

Pradok Sparrow	Mexico
Skhug	Thailand
Biltong	United Kingdom
Mopani Worm	Japan
Stuffed Camel	Egypt
Blue Crab	Israel
Frog legs	Australia
Kushari	France
Lamb eyes	Saudi Arabia
Odori Ebi	United States of America
Agave Honey	Canada
Flossy Pork	South Africa
Guinness Pie	Zimbabwe

Some facts about delicacies and delicacy providers.

Did you know that...?

- The balut to a Filipino is best served when it is seventeen days old. It is eaten as just one of the stages from egg to duck.
- The eyes of a lamb's are often given to honored guests in Saudi Arabia.
- Domestic pigs were brought to southeastern North America from Europe by De Soto and other early Spanish explorers.
- Alligator meat is considered cooked when it is white all the way through.
- Wealthy Chinese patronize more restaurants that openly serve cat and dog meat often as a specialty.
- Chinese strongly believe that eating Virgin Boy Eggs improves blood circulation and lower body heat.
- Monkeys express affection and pacify others by grooming each other.
- The zebra caterpillar becomes poisonous by eating poisonous foods, while the butterfly smells very bad.
- The pangolin's tongue when fully extended can be up to 16 inches long.
- The needle in Alexander Graham Bell's first photograph was made of bamboo.

- A chicken will lay bigger and stronger eggs if you change the lighting in such a way as to make them think a day is 28 hours long.
- A rooster will attack anything that he thinks will harm the hens.
- Iguanas are the largest in the lizard family.
- Turtle shells are made from 60 different bones all connected together and can feel you touching it because it has nerves in its shell.
- Sturgeon roe, or caviar, is the best-known and most expensive in most restaurants menu in the U.S.A.
- Offal includes the heart, liver, tongue, lungs, spleen, kidneys, bone marrow, testicles, brain, mesentery (intestinal membrane), feet, sweetbreads, stomach, oxtail, pig snouts, and head.
- The Ostrich has the largest eyes of any land animal. Its eye measures almost 2 inches (5 cm) across.
- The top two rows of a cat's whiskers can move independently of the lower two rows. This allows maximum perception of the cat's immediate surroundings.
- A python usually eats only 4 to 5 times in a year.
- The official state plant of Texas is the edible prickly pear cactus.
- Frogs absorb water through their skin, so they don't need to drink.
- In some species the worker ants also lay infertile eggs to serve as food for the larvae.
- Fast food hamburgers come from culled dairy cows.
- One portabella mushroom has more potassium than a banana.

- To treat digestive problems, Greeks would eat ginger wrapped in bread.

In conclusion, this book has taken you on a journey around the world of delicacies. I hope you now really understand and respect what other people consider to eat and what they consider to be delicacies. People around the world have their cultural reasons to partake certain foods as delicacies. I repeat the English adage which states that "One man's meat is another man's poison". This saying fits very well in the world's different cultural delicacies. It is important to respect one's delicacy and they will in turn respect yours this may help us leave in peace and harmony all the world. I find it appalling for someone who eats stink bug to despise that one who eats frog legs, dog meat, and pig brain, crab, and baboon or drink cow urine as a soft-drink or soda. I have found that all delicacies in this contribution have some nutritional or medicinal values. I feel all we need is an education into each other's food and delicacies then we will be able to appreciate global delicacies. It does not necessarily mean we should eat other peoples' delicacies. All we need is an educated insight into those delicacies. I feel one has a choice to taste, if need be, such delicacies other than theirs'. My folks do not eat most sea foods like lobster, crabs, shrimp and others. The reason is very simple; we have no access to such food since our country is landlocked. When I came to the United States of America, I unwillingly sampled such foods. I enjoy eating shrimp, though it is expensive. I have also learnt that some people do not eat certain delicacies because of their scarcity and prohibitive prices. Some people are superstitious and attach unproven cultural theories towards certain foods. In culture we say," Chekudya chose marimba waraira, meaning you may taste any food then make a choice and decision, whether you like or not.

References.

Doctorow C, 2011 Context (Excerpt) Tachyon Publishers, San Francisco

Eric L, 1996 Smoketrack Lightning: Adventures in the Heart of Barbecue Country, New York Times

Cunningham L.J. et al 2001 A History of Guam, Guam Publishing, Honolulu

BBQ and Bourbon: How to Barbecue A Cow's Head: May 2009

Food Tease: Cow Head Barbecue: September, 2009

Food and Agriculture Organization of the United Nations: Pumpkin: South Pacific Commission: 1986"

Leblon Finatinas Para, Guam Cookbook, Y Ineton Famalaoan,1988

Recipe Tips: Pumpkin Leaves, Cooked, Boiled, Drained, With Salt

AfriChef: South African Recipes

Leaf for Life: Green Leaf Recipes

The Times: Urban Farmer—Sweet corn Surprise

Aavi's Recipes: Cabbage Vada

Sinclair's in Zimbabwe-Crocodile Farm: http://www.youtube.com/watch?v=exKIposeCt0

A Visit to a Zimbabwe Crocodile Farm: http://www.nowpublic.com/world/mopane-worms#ixzzIzshsvr5Q

Mopani Worms :http://www.nowpublic.com/world/mopane-worms

How to Cook Kapenta Fish: http://www.livestrong.com/article/53730I-how-to-cook-kapenta-fish/#ixzz20RCBZymS

How to Cook Kapenta Fish: http://www.livestrong.com/article/53730I-how-to-cook-kapenta-fish/#ixzz20RGmjASt

How to Cook Kapenta Fish: http://www.livestrong.com/article/53730I-how-to-cook-kapenta-fish/#ixzz20RClnujk

How to Cook Kapenta Fish: http://www.livestrong.com/article/53730I-how-to-cook-kapenta-fish/#ixzz20RHK6WXH

Recipe ;Egg Pork Brains Internet Cookbook: http://www.virtualcities.com/ons/nc/gov/ncgvhcI.htm

Eating Pig Brain-YouTube video: http://www.youtube.com/watch?v=KmnXImydXrk

Fancy a Bowl of Jiggly Pig Brain Soup:http://eastcoastlife.blogspot.com/2010/0I/fancy-bowl-of-jiggly-pig-brain-soup-ph.html

Eat Your Bugs-Harvesting Edible Stink-Bugs :http://www.scienceinafrica.co.za/2003/october/stinkbug.htm

How to Cook a Cow Foot: http://www.livestrong.com/article/470847-how-to-cook-a-cow-foot/#ixzzIztbbzgd

How to Cook a Cow's Head: http://www.livestrong.com/article/473666-how-to-cook-a-cows-head/#ixzzIzv7phdq9

How to Cook a Cow's Head: http://www.livestrong.com/article/473666-how-to-cook-a-cows-head/#ixzzIzv6kb8Z7

How to Cook Beef Intestines: http://www.livestrong.com/article/463559-how-to-cook-beef-intestines/#ixzzIzv9OJBkA

How to Cook Lamb Intestines: http://www.livestrong.com/article/489416-how-to-cook-lamb-intestines/#ixzz208WaRTUA

http://images.search.yahoo.com/search/images?_adv_prop=image&fr=yfp-t-70I-I4&sz=all&va=goat+gut

How to Cook Tripe: How to Cook Tripe | eHow.com http://www.ehow.com/how_2079856_cook-tripe.html#ixzzIzvDp26Lg

How to Cook Chicken Feet: http://search.yahoo.com/search;_ylt=AugQBU65DdiWFNZId4pM57WbvZx4?fr=yfp-t-70I-I4-s&toggle=I&cop=mss&ei=UTF-8&p=picture%20of%20chicken%20feet

Rabbit Recipes: http://www.bowhunting.net/susieq/rabbit.html

How to Catch a Mouse: http://www.ehow.com/how_2I60I77_catch-a-mouse.html#ixzz20G5wHM5J

Mark Blumberg's South Africa Biltong Recipe Page: http://www.markblumberg.com/biltong.html

Giant Pangolin-Facts and Pictures: http://thewebsiteofeverything. com/animals/mammals/Pholidota/Manidae/Manis/ Manis-gigantea.html

How to Cook Pumpkin Leaves: http://www.livestrong. com/article/468239-how-to-cook-pumpkin- leaves/#ixzz20C5YsGmd

How to Cook Pumpkin Leaves: http://www.livestrong. com/article/468239-how-to-cook-pumpkin- leaves/#ixzz20C6xviPz

How to Cook Pumpkin Leaves: http://www.livestrong. com/article/468239-how-to-cook-pumpkin- leaves/#ixzz20C6lonu8

China's Urine –Boiled Eggs A Cultural Delicacy: http://gizmodo. com/5897678/chinas-urine+boiled-eggs-are-a-cultural- delicacy

Hindu Extremists Promote Cow- Urine Soft-Drink: http:// boingboing.net/2009/02/12/hindu-extremists-pro.html

Asia Travel: 10 Unusual Asian Delicacies: http://unearthingasia. com/feature-highlights/10-unusual-asian-delicacies/

LiveLeak.com- Snake Meat, A Popular Delicacy Among Tribals: http://www.liveleak.com/view?i=847_1208105057

Can a Rattle Snake be Eaten Safely: http://voices.yahoo.com/can- rattlesnake-meat-eaten-safely-5718906.html?cat=58

How to Cook Grasshoppers the Mexican Way.

http://www.instructables.com/id/How-to-cook-Grasshoppers-
the-Mexican-way/

How to Prepare Deep Fried Crispy Pig Intestines

http://peteformation.blogspot.com/2010/08/how-to-cook-
deep-fried-crispy-pig.html

Algae and Recipes.

http://www.simplyrecipes.com/recipes/kale_with_seaweed_
sesame_and_ginger/

http://science.yourdictionary.com/articles/what-eats-algae.html

http://search.yahoo.com/search;_ylt=A0oG7t7qkq9QBT8
AuDlXNyoA?p=algae%20eaters%20%20as%20a%20
delicacy&fr2=sb-top&fr=yfp-t-701-s .

http://www.oilgae.com/

How Prepare Shrimps and Prawns.

http://www.bestprawnrecipes.com/fingerlicking-prawn-recipe/

http://www.shrimprecipe.org/shrimp_dip_recipe.html